# THE
# Vegan
# Holiday
## COOKBOOK

# THE
# Vegan
# Holiday
## COOKBOOK

From Elegant Appetizers
to Festive Mains and
Delicious Sweets

# Marie Laforêt

Robert
ROSE

*Many thanks to Mathieu for his invaluable help*
*while I was writing this book.*

**The Vegan Holiday Cookbook**
Originally published under the titles *Noël Vegan* © 2015, Éditions la Plage (Paris) and
*Joyeux Noël Vegan* © 2016, Éditions la Plage (Paris)
Translation copyright © 2017 Robert Rose Inc.
Cover and text design copyright © 2017 Robert Rose Inc.

*For complete cataloguing information, see page 144.*

**Disclaimer**
The recipes in this book have been carefully tested by our kitchen and our tasters. To the best of our knowledge, they are safe and nutritious for ordinary use and users. For those people with food or other allergies, or who have special food requirements or health issues, please read the suggested contents of each recipe carefully and determine whether or not they may create a problem for you. All recipes are used at the risk of the consumer.

We cannot be responsible for any hazards, loss or damage that may occur as a result of any recipe use.

For those with special needs, allergies, requirements or health problems, in the event of any doubt, please contact your medical adviser prior to the use of any recipe.

Translator: Donna Vekteris
Editors: Sue Sumeraj and Jennifer MacKenzie
Proofreader: Kelly Jones
Indexer: Gillian Watts
Design and production: Alicia McCarthy & Kevin Cockburn/PageWave Graphics Inc.
Photography: Marie Laforêt

Published by Robert Rose Inc.
120 Eglinton Avenue East, Suite 800, Toronto, Ontario, Canada M4P 1E2
Tel: (416) 322-6552 Fax: (416) 322-6936
www.robertrose.ca

Printed and bound in Canada

1 2 3 4 5 6 7 8 9 TCP 25 24 23 22 21 20 19 18 17

# Contents

# Introduction

◆

**The special meals served during holidays are often real challenges for vegans** — and for non-vegans who wish to reduce their consumption of animal products. There is a great deal of social pressure to offer guests a traditional meat-laden menu at this time of year. The weight of tradition can seem oppressive at times.

Imagine another kind of holiday — one where we celebrate ideas and values that are dear to us, like justice and compassion, while enjoying cuisine that is ethical without sacrificing elegance. A meal where there is no requirement to conform to the tradition of consuming turkey, beef or salmon just because that's what your family has always served for the holiday. A feast that focuses on being together and sharing the same foods, with no one excluded.

This kind of holiday is no utopian dream, but my gift to you: more than 60 festive recipes that will be enjoyed by both vegans and non-vegans alike. You will discover innovative substitutes for those time-honored meat, fish and cheese dishes, new versions of glazed logs and chocolates, and recipes for gourmet gifts your guests will adore.

Vegan cuisine does not require that we do away with our traditions; rather, it allows those traditions to evolve and become ethical without sacrificing flavor, so we can all enjoy celebrating together and sharing good times and good food.

# A Gluten-Free Holiday

**Eating vegan during holiday festivities is not always easy, and if you are also gluten-intolerant, it can be very complicated.** That's why I've attempted to eliminate or reduce gluten in many of the recipes in this book. To make it even easier for you, I've listed them here in different categories: recipes that are gluten-free, recipes that are easy to adapt, and recipes that are more difficult to adapt but that you can test if you feel like experimenting.

## GLUTEN-FREE

- Nordic Terrine (serve with gluten-free bread)
- Caviar Trio (serve with gluten-free bread)
- Vegan Taramasalata
- Fisherman's Rillettes
- Saint Jacques–Style Shiitake Bites
- Squash Truffles
- Shiitake Mushroom and White Bean Soup (make sure your miso is gluten-free)
- Tofu Medallions with Duxelles and Squash (make sure your miso is gluten-free)
- Sweet Potatoes Stuffed with Chestnuts and Smoked Tempeh
- Porcini Mushroom Risotto (make sure your broth is gluten-free)
- Roasted Beets and Onions with Horseradish Dill Sauce
- Pommes Duchesse
- Hasselback Potatoes with Homemade Sage Butter
- Potato Kohlrabi Pancakes
- Chestnut Crème Brûlée
- Mont Blanc–Style Panna Cotta (make sure your confectioners' sugar is gluten-free)
- Citrus Mini Pavlovas (make sure your confectioners' sugar is gluten-free)
- Glazed Pear, Caramel and Chocolate Pavlova (make sure your confectioners' sugar is gluten-free)
- Vanilla Raspberry Vacherin (make sure your confectioners' sugar is gluten-free)
- White Chocolate Medallions
- Pecan, Pumpkin Seed and Cranberry Medallions
- Coriander and Olive Oil Truffles (make sure your confectioners' sugar is gluten-free)
- Coconut Truffles

## EASY TO ADAPT

- Quick Foie Gras-Style Mousse: Use gluten-free bread for the toast
- Tofu Gravlax Canapés: Use gluten-free bread for the toast
- Mozzarella Cranberry Croquettes: Use gluten-free bread crumbs
- Chestnut Vol-au-Vents: Use Gluten-Free Vegan Puff Pastry (page 41)
- Cream of Leek Turnovers: Use Gluten-Free Vegan Puff Pastry (page 41) and make sure your miso is gluten-free
- Puff Pastry Stars with Chestnut and Sweet Potato Filling: Use Gluten-Free Vegan Puff Pastry (page 41)
- Ravioli in Flavored Broth: Use gluten-free ravioli pasta and make sure your miso is gluten-free
- Holiday Roast: Make sure your rusks, broth and miso are gluten-free
- Fisherman's Puff Pastries: Use Gluten-Free Vegan Puff Pastry (page 41)

## MORE DIFFICULT TO ADAPT

- Mushroom Vegetable Crumble: Test with a gluten-free flour mixture in place of the whole wheat flour
- Herbed Potato Waffles: Test with a gluten-free flour mixture in place of the bread flour
- Snow White Layer Cake: Test with a gluten-free flour mixture in place of the all-purpose flour and make sure your baking powder and confectioners' sugar are gluten-free
- Orange Carrot Cake: Test with a gluten-free flour mixture in place of the all-purpose flour and make sure your baking powder and confectioners' sugar are gluten-free
- Marzipan Stollen: Test with a gluten-free flour mixture in place of the all-purpose flour and make sure your confectioners' sugar is gluten-free
- Cardamom Almond Kringle: Test with a gluten-free flour mixture in place of the all-purpose flour and make sure your confectioners' sugar is gluten-free
- Pepparkakor: Test with a gluten-free flour mixture in place of the all-purpose flour
- Shortbread Forest: Test with a gluten-free flour mixture in place of the bread flour and make sure your confectioners' sugar is gluten-free
- Glazed Citrus Meringue Log: Test with a gluten-free flour mixture in place of the all-purpose flour and make sure your baking powder and confectioners' sugar are gluten-free
- Almond Lemon Meringue Log: Test with a gluten-free flour mixture in place of the bread flour and make sure your confectioners' sugar is gluten-free

- Butternut Squash, Kale and Ricotta Cannelloni: Use gluten-free cannelloni pasta tubes
- Mushroom and Walnut Ravioli: Use tamari in place of soy sauce
- Mince Tarts: Use gluten-free pie dough and make sure your confectioners' sugar is gluten-free
- Mango Cocoa Domes: Use gluten-free cookies and make sure your confectioners' sugar is gluten-free
- Filled Chocolates: Use gluten-free cookies

# Holiday Menus

◆

**Looking for ideas for your holiday feast?** Using the recipes in this book, I have come up with four themed menus to help you set the perfect mood.

## TRADITIONAL

If you're looking for a meal with traditional, comforting wintertime flavors, this menu fits the bill.

- Nordic Terrine (page 16)
- Holiday Roast (page 57)
- Pommes Duchesse (page 85)
- Mozzarella Cranberry Croquettes (page 32) with green salad
- Vanilla Raspberry Vacherin (page 117)

## LIGHT AND SOPHISTICATED

If rustic dishes are not your cup of tea, this elegant menu will make your guests swoon but still leave them with an appetite the next day.

- Caviar Trio (page 23)
- Ravioli in Flavored Broth (page 54)
- Fisherman's Puff Pastries (page 69)
- Roasted Beets and Onions with Horseradish Dill Sauce (page 81)
- Almond Lemon Meringue Log (page 122)

## BUFFET

A buffet is ideal if you're expecting a crowd. It allows your guests to serve themselves according to their tastes and their appetite.

The focus is on recipes prepared as individual portions or that are easy to serve.

- Puff Pastry Stars with Chestnut and Sweet Potato Filling (page 47)
- Tofu Gravlax Canapés (page 27)
- Squash Truffles (page 35)
- Chestnut, Mushroom and Hazelnut Paupiettes (page 66)
- Swedish Meatballs with Mustard Dill Sauce (page 65)
- Hasselback Potatoes with Homemade Sage Butter (page 86)
- Porcini Mushroom Risotto (page 78)
- Snow White Layer Cake (page 94)

## LAST-MINUTE

If you have only a few days' notice and no time to cook on the day of the party, these recipes will help you put together an impressive feast in very little time.

- Quick Foie Gras–Style Mousse on Paris Toasts (page 24)
- Saint Jacques–Style Shiitake Bites (page 31)
- Tofu Medallions with Duxelles and Squash (page 62)
- Citrus Mini Pavlovas (page 113) or Mango Cocoa Domes (page 125)

# Elegant Appetizers

## SPREADS

Foie Gras–Style Terrine
12

Tofu Terrine with Porcini
Mushrooms and Walnuts
15

Nordic Terrine
16

Vegan Taramasalata
19

Fisherman's Rillettes
20

## HORS D'OEUVRES

Caviar Trio
23

Quick Foie Gras–Style
Mousse on Paris Toasts
24

Tofu Gravlax Canapés
27

Blinis with Carrot Gravlax
28

Saint Jacques–Style
Shiitake Bites
31

Mozzarella Cranberry
Croquettes
32

Squash Truffles
35

Potato and Vegan Cheese
Tartes Fines
36

Vegan Sausage Mini Tarts
39

Classic Vegan Puff Pastry
40

Gluten-Free Vegan Puff Pastry
41

Chestnut Vol-au-Vents
43

Cream of Leek Turnovers
44

Puff Pastry Stars with Chestnut
and Sweet Potato Filling
47

# Foie Gras–Style Terrine

This vegan version of foie gras does not pretend to be a faithful imitation,
but it is an ethical alternative that can be used in recipes that call for foie gras.
It is also delicious spread on Paris toasts.

◆

## MAKES 8 SERVINGS

- Immersion blender
- Terrine dish, ramekins or small metal pastry rings

| | | |
|---|---|---|
| 7 oz | shiitake mushrooms, stems trimmed, thinly sliced | 200 g |
| 1 tbsp | olive oil | 15 mL |
| 4 oz | silken tofu | 125 g |
| 2 tsp | agar-agar powder | 6 g |
| 2/3 cup | soy cream | 150 mL |
| 1 to 2 tbsp | Armagnac or cognac | 15 to 30 mL |
| 1/2 tsp | salt | 3 g |
| 1/4 tsp | freshly ground black pepper | 0.5 g |
| 1/4 tsp | ground coriander | 0.5 g |
| Pinch | ground nutmeg | Pinch |
| Pinch | ground cloves | Pinch |
| 1/2 cup | melted virgin coconut oil | 125 mL |
| 1/4 cup | white miso | 60 mL |
| 1/4 cup | walnut oil | 60 mL |

1. In a skillet over medium heat, sauté mushrooms in olive oil for about 8 minutes. Add tofu and use immersion blender to blend mushrooms and tofu.

2. In a small saucepan, combine agar-agar, soy cream and Armagnac; bring to a boil and cook, stirring, for 2 minutes.

3. Add the cream mixture to the tofu mixture. Add salt, pepper, coriander, nutmeg, cloves, coconut oil, miso and walnut oil; blend again.

4. Transfer to terrine dish and let set in refrigerator for 4 hours.

# Tofu Terrine

## with Porcini Mushrooms and Walnuts

This rich, firm but soft terrine is filled with delicate morsels of porcini mushrooms and walnuts. Add a touch of elegance to this rustic spread with a few sprouts, capers or pickles on the side.

◆

### MAKES 4 TO 6 SERVINGS

- Terrine dish, lined with plastic wrap

| | | |
|---|---|---|
| ½ cup | dried porcini mushroom pieces | 16 g |
| | Warm water | |
| 3 tbsp | olive oil | 45 mL |
| 2 | cloves garlic, minced | 2 |
| 1 | onion, minced | 1 |
| 8 oz | firm tofu, diced | 250 g |
| ⅓ cup | chopped walnuts | 40 g |
| 1 tbsp | soy sauce | 15 mL |
| ½ cup | chickpea flour | 50 g |
| ½ tsp | garlic powder | 1 g |
| Pinch | Chinese five-spice powder | Pinch |
| ¾ cup + 5 tsp | water | 200 mL |
| 1 tsp | barley miso | 5 mL |
| 1 tbsp | finely chopped fresh chives | 3 g |
| | Salt and freshly ground black pepper | |

1. Rehydrate porcini mushrooms in a bowl of warm water for 20 minutes; drain well.

2. In a skillet, heat oil over medium heat. Add mushrooms, garlic, onion and tofu; sauté for 5 minutes, stirring often with a wooden spatula and crushing mixture to the texture of stuffing. Add walnuts and soy sauce; cook for 5 minutes, crushing mixture as much as possible. Remove from heat.

3. In a small saucepan, combine chickpea flour, garlic powder, five-spice powder, water and miso. Cook over medium heat, stirring constantly, until mixture thickens and turns sticky.

4. Transfer miso mixture to skillet, add chives and season to taste with salt and pepper. Cook over low heat, stirring well, for a few minutes to blend the flavors.

5. Transfer mixture to prepared terrine dish and let set in refrigerator for 2 hours.

# Nordic Terrine

Inspired by Norwegian *fisk pate* ("fish paste"), this sea-flavored terrine with tiny vegetables is sure to astonish your guests. Serve with Paris toasts and lemon wedges on the side for squeezing.

◆

## MAKES 8 SERVINGS

- Immersion blender
- Small cake mold, lined with plastic wrap or lightly oiled

| | | |
|---|---|---|
| 14 oz | soft smoked tofu | 400 g |
| 2 | carrots, chopped and cooked in water | 2 |
| Pinch | garlic powder | Pinch |
| Pinch | freshly ground black pepper | Pinch |
| ¼ cup | melted virgin coconut oil | 60 mL |
| 3 tbsp | freshly squeezed lemon juice | 45 mL |
| 2 tbsp | flaked seaweed seasoning | 3 g |
| 1¼ cups | water | 300 mL |
| ¾ tsp | agar-agar powder | 2 g |
| ½ cup | finely chopped fennel, cooked in water | 50 g |
| ⅓ cup | baby green peas, cooked in water | 50 g |
| 1 tsp | dried dillweed (or 2 tsp/2 g chopped fresh dill) | 1 g |

## TIP

Tofu differs in taste and texture from one brand to another. For this recipe, it is better to use a fairly soft tofu. Firmer tofu does not have the right texture for a terrine.

1. In a bowl, combine tofu, carrots, garlic powder, pepper, coconut oil and lemon juice; blend with the immersion blender until texture is smooth and consistent.

2. In a small saucepan, combine seaweed seasoning and water; bring to a boil. Remove from heat and let steep for a few minutes, then strain to collect ⅔ cup (150 mL) seaweed broth.

3. Return broth to saucepan, add agar-agar and bring to a boil. Cook, stirring, for 30 seconds.

4. Add seaweed jelly to tofu mixture and blend until smooth. Stir in fennel, peas and dill.

5. Transfer terrine to prepared cake mold, smooth the top and let set in refrigerator for 7 hours. Gently unmold terrine onto a dish.

# Vegan Taramasalata

This simple recipe is sure to delight your vegan and non-vegan guests with a texture and flavor that are surprisingly similar to the original Greek seafood spread. This spread is ideal on blinis or Swedish flatbread (*polarbröd*), with lemon wedges on the side for squeezing at the last minute.

---

## MAKES 6 SERVINGS

- Immersion blender (see tip)

| | | |
|---|---|---|
| ¾ cup + 5 tsp | soy cream | 200 mL |
| 2 tbsp | flaked seaweed seasoning | 3 g |
| 2½ oz | firm smoked tofu, crumbled | 75 g |
| 2 tbsp | plain soy yogurt | 30 mL |
| 2 tbsp | tomato paste | 30 mL |
| 1 tbsp | freshly squeezed lemon juice | 15 mL |
| 2 tbsp | chia seeds | 24 g |
| Pinch | salt | Pinch |

### TIP

If you don't have an immersion blender, you can transfer the cream mixture to a regular blender after step 1 and proceed to blend as in step 2.

1. In a small saucepan, combine soy cream and seaweed seasoning; heat over high heat for a few minutes, stirring constantly.

2. Using the immersion blender in the pan, blend until creamy. Add tofu, yogurt, tomato paste and lemon juice; blend until very creamy.

3. Transfer to a bowl and stir in chia seeds and salt; let stand for 30 minutes. Refrigerate until ready to serve.

# Fisherman's Rillettes

For several years I've been focusing on recipes from the sea, which can be tricky to reproduce in vegan cuisine. I'm proud to say that these soft and creamy rillettes are one of my best culinary discoveries. This is the kind of simple, inexpensive but impressive recipe you'll be happy to serve all year round.

## MAKES 4 SERVINGS

• Terrine dish or ramekins

| | | |
|---|---|---|
| 1 cup + 6 tbsp | drained cooked white beans (see tip) | 250 g |
| 4 oz | extra-firm smoked tofu (see tip) | 125 g |
| 1½ tbsp | flaked seaweed seasoning | 2.5 g |
| 3 tbsp | vegan margarine | 42 g |
| 3 tbsp | freshly squeezed lemon juice | 45 mL |
| | Salt and freshly ground black pepper | |

## TIPS

There are a variety of brands of smoked tofu. They all have different consistencies, and I use them in different ways depending on the recipe. In this case, it is necessary to use extra-firm smoked tofu, which is slightly brown on the outside.

When preparing the beans for this recipe, cook them until very soft.

1. In a bowl, mash beans with a fork. Crumble tofu by hand into the bowl and combine with the beans. Add seaweed seasoning, margarine and lemon juice, mashing with a fork. Season to taste with salt and pepper.

2. Press mixture into terrine dish and refrigerate for at least 2 hours before serving.

# Caviar Trio

Thanks to the magic of molecular cooking, it's very easy to create tiny beads of vegan caviar. You'll find three different recipes here that you can make separately or combine for more variety. Serve with Homemade Vegan Crème Fraîche (page 27) on Paris toasts or blinis.

## MAKES 1 SMALL BOWL OF EACH CAVIAR

- Fine-mesh sieve
- Syringe

| | | |
|---|---|---|
| 1 cup | neutral vegetable oil | 250 mL |

### Classic Caviar

| | | |
|---|---|---|
| 1 cup | water | 250 mL |
| 2 tbsp | flaked seaweed seasoning | 3 g |
| 1½ tbsp | tamari | 22 mL |
| ¾ tsp | agar-agar powder | 2 g |

### Smoked Seafood Caviar

| | | |
|---|---|---|
| 3 tbsp + 1 tsp | carrot juice | 50 mL |
| ¾ cup + 5 tsp | water | 200 mL |
| 1½ tsp | smoked paprika | 3 g |
| 2 tsp | flaked seaweed seasoning | 1 g |
| Pinch | salt | Pinch |
| ¾ tsp | agar-agar powder | 2 g |

### Mushroom Caviar

| | | |
|---|---|---|
| 1 cup | water | 250 mL |
| 2 tbsp | finely chopped dried porcini mushrooms | 5 g |
| 2 tsp | minced garlic | 10 g |
| 1 tbsp | chopped parsley | 4 g |
| ¾ tsp | agar-agar powder | 2 g |

1. Pour oil into a glass and chill in refrigerator for 3 to 4 hours before making caviar. Oil must be very cold.

2. In a small saucepan, mix all ingredients (except agar-agar) for one type of caviar and bring to a boil. Let ingredients steep for 1 to 2 minutes to give the broth more flavor.

3. Use a fine-mesh sieve to strain broth into a small bowl, then whisk in agar-agar. Return to saucepan and bring to a boil. Stir for 30 seconds, then return mixture to the bowl.

4. Use a syringe to extract mixture and squeeze one droplet at a time into glass of oil. The droplets will form tiny beads that will cool on contact with the cold oil and turn to jelly as they sink to the bottom.

5. Once all caviar is made, use a fine-mesh sieve to strain the oil and collect the beads. Immerse beads in a large bowl of water. Remaining oil will rise to the surface. Strain water from bowl through a fine-mesh sieve to collect the caviar. Keep refrigerated until ready to serve.

# Quick Foie Gras–Style Mousse on Paris Toasts

Here's a great recipe if you need to come up with a first course at the last minute. This smooth and satisfying mousse stands in for foie gras without trying to perfectly imitate it. You can also use it as a puff pastry filling or in gourmet terrines.

## MAKES 4 TO 6 SERVINGS

- Immersion blender or food processor
- Pastry bag fitted with a fluted piping tip

| | | |
|---|---|---|
| 2 tbsp | chopped dried porcini mushrooms | 5 g |
| ¼ cup | broken dried shiitake mushrooms | 10 g |
| | Warm water | |
| 7 oz | firm tofu, crumbled | 200 g |
| ¼ cup | softened virgin coconut oil | 60 mL |
| 2 tbsp | sweet white wine | 30 mL |
| 1 tbsp | tamari | 15 mL |
| Pinch | freshly ground black pepper | Pinch |
| Pinch | salt | Pinch |
| Pinch | gingerbread spice (or to taste) | Pinch |
| | Paris toasts | |

1. Rehydrate porcini and shiitake mushrooms in a bowl of warm water for 20 minutes. Drain and reserve 1 tbsp (15 mL) soaking water.

2. Place tofu in immersion blender cup or food processor. Add rehydrated mushrooms, reserved soaking water, coconut oil, wine, tamari, pepper, salt and gingerbread spice. Process until texture is very fine and consistent.

3. Transfer mixture to a pastry bag and refrigerate until ready to serve. Use pastry bag to decorate Paris toasts with mousse.

# Tofu Gravlax Canapés

A marinade inspired by Swedish gravlax transforms simple tofu into delicate canapés, for a simple but inspired recipe. The gravlax can also be used in salads, on bagels or in sandwiches the rest of the year!

◆

## MAKES 4 SERVINGS

- Mandoline
- Fine-mesh sieve

| | | |
|---|---|---|
| 3½ oz | soft tofu | 100 g |
| | Paris toasts | |
| 2 | lemon wedges (optional) | 2 |

### Marinade

| | | |
|---|---|---|
| 1½ tbsp | pink peppercorns | 9 g |
| 1 tbsp | white peppercorns | 13 g |
| 1 tbsp | chopped fresh dill | 3 g |
| 1 tbsp | raw cane sugar | 12 g |
| 1 tbsp | smoked salt | 15 g |
| ½ tsp | smoked paprika | 1 g |
| 3 tbsp | freshly squeezed lemon juice | 45 mL |
| 1 tbsp | walnut oil | 15 mL |
| 1 to 2 tsp | beet juice | 5 to 10 mL |

### Homemade Vegan Crème Fraîche

| | | |
|---|---|---|
| 7 oz | plain soy yogurt | 200 g |
| ¾ cup + 5 tsp | thick soy cream | 200 mL |

1. Place tofu between two plates, add a weight on top and press for 1 hour. (This will help drain the tofu and will allow the marinade to be absorbed more easily.)

2. *Marinade:* In a dish, combine pink and white peppercorns, dill, sugar, salt, paprika, lemon juice, walnut oil and beet juice.

3. Using a mandoline, slice tofu very thinly. Add to marinade and let stand for 1 to 2 hours. Remove tofu from marinade and drain in a fine-mesh sieve.

4. *Vegan Crème Fraîche:* In a small bowl, combine yogurt and soy cream.

5. Spoon a little crème fraîche on Paris toasts and top with 1 or 2 thin slices of tofu. If desired, squeeze a little lemon juice on top.

## TIP

Tofu differs in taste and texture from one brand to another. For this recipe, it is better to use a fairly soft tofu.

# Blinis with Carrot Gravlax

Here's a fresh, healthy and ethical alternative to gravlax that maintains the color and aromatic flavors of the famous Swedish salmon dish.

◆

## MAKES 20 BLINIS

- Mandoline

### Carrot Gravlax

| | | |
|---|---|---|
| 2 | medium carrots | 2 |
| 1½ tsp | chopped fresh dill | 2 g |
| 1 tsp | salt | 6 g |
| ½ tsp | raw cane sugar | 2 g |
| ½ tsp | crushed white peppercorns | 2 g |
| ½ tsp | pink peppercorns | 1 g |

### Blinis

| | | |
|---|---|---|
| 1½ cups | all-purpose flour | 200 g |
| 2 tsp | quick-rising (instant) yeast | 7 g |
| 2 tsp | cornstarch | 6 g |
| ½ tsp | raw cane sugar | 2 g |
| Pinch | salt (or to taste) | Pinch |
| 7 oz | plain soy yogurt | 200 g |
| 2 tsp | almond milk | 10 mL |
| ¾ tsp | neutral vegetable oil | 3 mL |
| | Additional neutral vegetable oil | |

### Accompaniments

| | | |
|---|---|---|
| 1 cup | Homemade Vegan Crème Fraîche (page 27) or vegan sour cream | 250 g |
| 2 | lemons, cut into small wedges | 2 |

1. *Gravlax:* Peel carrots. Using a mandoline, slice carrots very thinly lengthwise.

2. In a small bowl or dish, combine carrots, dill, salt, sugar, white peppercorns and pink peppercorns. Let marinate for 12 hours.

3. *Blinis:* In a small bowl, combine flour, yeast, cornstarch, sugar and salt. Whisk in yogurt, almond milk and oil until very smooth.

4. Heat an oiled skillet over medium heat. Drop a spoonful of batter into skillet and cook for 1 minute per side. Transfer blini to a plate. Repeat with the remaining batter, oiling the skillet and adjusting the heat as necessary between batches.

5. When ready to serve, spread a little crème fraîche on each blini and top with gravlax. Garnish plates with lemon wedges, to be squeezed just before eating.

# Saint Jacques–Style Shiitake Bites

Chefs often rely on mushrooms in vegan cuisine, as their texture makes them the ideal substitute for shellfish. I like using shiitake mushrooms, which have a very mild flavor. Combined with a little seaweed to give them a briny note, they take on a flavor reminiscent of scallops.

## MAKES 4 SERVINGS

- 1¼-inch (3 cm) round cookie cutter

| | | |
|---|---|---|
| 1 | sheet yaki nori | 1 |
| ¾ cup + 5 tsp | water | 200 mL |
| 12 | medium shiitake mushrooms, stems removed | 12 |
| 1½ tbsp | olive oil, divided | 22 mL |
| 1 tsp | sesame oil | 5 mL |
| 2 tbsp | white wine | 30 mL |
| 1 tsp | chopped fresh chives (optional) | 1 g |
| 1 tsp | chopped fresh dill (optional) | 1 g |
| 6 tbsp + 2 tsp | soy cream | 100 mL |
| | Salt and freshly ground black pepper | |

## TIP

These little mushroom bites are perfect with a salad on the side.

1. Cut yaki nori sheet into large pieces and boil in water for about 2 minutes. Strain and set aside 6 tbsp + 2 tsp (100 mL) seaweed concentrate.

2. Using the cookie cutter, cut out circles from the center of each mushroom. (Save the leftover mushroom from the outer ring for another recipe.) Gently remove thin brown skin on top of mushroom circles.

3. In a skillet, heat 1 tbsp (15 mL) olive oil and sesame oil over high heat. Brown one side of mushrooms, then the other side, adding the rest of the olive oil. Add seaweed concentrate, 1 tbsp (15 mL) at a time, until it is completely absorbed. Immediately transfer to individual dishes or a platter.

4. Add wine, scraping up any brown bits from the bottom of the pan. Stir in chives (if using), dill (if using) and soy cream. Season to taste with salt and pepper. Serve with shiitake mushrooms.

# Mozzarella Cranberry Croquettes

The crispy and tender little morsels known as croquettes lend themselves especially well to vegan cuisine. In this version, I added cranberries and chives to vegan mozzarella for a sweet and savory mixture that is sure to please everyone. You can use this recipe as a base to make other types of croquettes.

◆

## MAKES 6 SERVINGS

| | | |
|---|---|---|
| 14 oz | vegan mozzarella | 400 g |
| 1/3 cup | chopped fresh chives | 16 g |
| 1/3 cup | chopped dried cranberries | 50 g |
| 1/2 tsp | garlic powder | 1 g |
| | Salt and freshly ground black pepper | |
| 2/3 cup | cornstarch | 85 g |
| 2/3 cup | water | 150 mL |
| 2 1/3 cups | dry bread crumbs | 250 g |
| 2 cups | neutral vegetable oil | 500 mL |

## TIPS

It is fairly easy to find vegan mozzarella in well-stocked supermarkets and natural foods stores. You may not enjoy eating it on its own, but it is great in cooked recipes — especially this one.

This recipe also makes the perfect substitute for the traditional cheese course. Pair with a green salad and serve after the main course and before dessert.

1. In a medium bowl, mash mozzarella, then stir in chives, cranberries and garlic powder. Season to taste with salt and pepper. Form mixture into small balls and set aside.

2. In a small bowl, combine cornstarch and water. Spread bread crumbs on a plate. Dip a mozzarella ball in cornstarch mixture, then roll in bread crumbs. Repeat to create a very thick coating. Set aside. Coat all balls in the same way.

3. In a small saucepan, heat oil over medium heat. Add 2 croquettes, ensuring that they are completely covered in oil, and cook until browned. Using a slotted spoon, transfer croquettes to a plate lined with paper towel to absorb excess oil. Repeat with the remaining croquettes. Serve hot.

# Squash Truffles

What could be more elegant than truffles? Here is a savory version made with squash. Paired with a winter salad, it also makes an impressive first course.

◆

## MAKES 15 TO 20 TRUFFLES

- Food processor

| | | |
|---|---|---|
| 7 oz | peeled butternut squash or pie pumpkin, cut into cubes | 200 g |
| Pinch | gingerbread spice (or to taste) | Pinch |
| Pinch | salt | Pinch |
| Pinch | freshly ground black pepper | Pinch |
| Pinch | garlic powder | Pinch |
| ¼ cup | melted virgin coconut oil | 60 mL |
| 2 tbsp | gluten-free white miso | 30 mL |
| 1 tbsp | truffle olive oil | 15 mL |
| 2 tbsp | sesame seeds | 18 g |
| 5 | gluten-free crispbreads, finely crumbled | 5 |

### TIP

If you can find Potimarron squash, a French heirloom variety of winter squash (also called Hokkaido or Kuri), it would be wonderful in this recipe.

1. Steam squash until soft, then pat dry to remove any excess moisture.

2. In food processor, combine squash, gingerbread spice, salt, pepper, garlic powder, coconut oil, miso and truffle olive oil; purée into a smooth cream. Freeze for 15 to 20 minutes.

3. In a skillet, toast sesame seeds for a few minutes. Mix with crumbled crispbread and transfer to a small dish.

4. Form 15 to 20 balls of squash mixture, then roll balls in crispbread mixture. Refrigerate until ready to serve.

# Potato and Vegan Cheese Tartes Fines

These sophisticated little melt-in-your-mouth tarts are both easy to make and economical. Try making them with sweet potatoes, butternut squash or celery root instead of potatoes. They stand on their own as hors d'oeuvres, but can also easily accompany a variety of dishes.

---

## MAKES 6 TO 8 TARTS

- Baking sheet, lined with parchment paper

### Dough

| | | |
|---|---|---|
| ¾ cup + 4 tsp | spelt flour | 100 g |
| ¾ cup | all-purpose flour | 100 g |
| 1 tsp | garlic powder | 3 g |
| 1 tsp | dried thyme | 1 g |
| ½ tsp | salt | 3 g |
| ¼ cup | olive oil | 60 mL |
| ⅓ cup | water | 80 mL |

### Topping

| | | |
|---|---|---|
| 7 to 8 oz | vegan mozzarella, thinly sliced | 200 to 250 g |
| 3 | medium potatoes, peeled and thinly sliced | 3 |
| 2 tsp | vegetable oil | 10 mL |
| | Salt and freshly ground black pepper | |
| 2 tsp | chopped fresh thyme | 1.5 g |

### TIPS

Vegan mozzarella is now fairly easy to find in well-stocked supermarkets and natural foods stores. Prefer a homemade version? Look for my recipe in *The Best Homemade Vegan Cheese and Ice Cream Recipes*.

Use a mandoline to slice the potatoes into thin rounds.

1. *Dough:* In a bowl, using your fingertips, combine spelt flour, all-purpose flour, garlic powder, thyme, salt and oil. Add water and knead to an even consistency. Form dough into a ball and refrigerate for 30 minutes.

2. Preheat oven to 350°F (180°C).

3. On a floured surface, roll dough out until thin. Cut out 6 to 8 circles and place on prepared baking sheet, spacing them evenly.

4. *Topping:* On each tart base, place a few mozzarella slices and 2 layers of potato slices. Oil lightly, then place 1 or 2 more mozzarella slices on top. Season with salt and pepper, then top with thyme.

5. Bake for about 20 minutes or until tarts are golden brown.

### VARIATION

Quick version: No time to make dough from scratch? Sprinkle a sheet of vegan pie dough with a little dried thyme and garlic powder. Lightly flour a rolling pin and roll it gently over the dough to press in the seasonings. Cut into circles for tarts.

# Vegan Sausage Mini Tarts

Dreaming of a simple, rustic meal with subtle and comforting flavors? This delectable recipe for mini vegan "meat pies" is meant for you! Serve hot or cold, as an appetizer or as a first course with a side salad. They also make a nice light meal the day after a big dinner.

◆

## MAKES 8 INDIVIDUAL TARTS

- Preheat oven to 325°F (160°C)
- Muffin pan, lightly oiled

| | | |
|---|---|---|
| 2 tbsp | olive oil | 30 mL |
| 3⅓ oz | vegan sausage | 100 g |
| 2 | shallots, finely chopped | 2 |
| ⅔ cup | frozen green peas | 100 g |
| 6 tbsp | finely chopped carrots | 50 g |
| 1½ tbsp | dried sage | 4.5 g |
| 6 tbsp + 2 tsp | soy cream | 100 mL |
| | Salt and freshly ground black pepper | |
| 1 | sheet vegan pie dough | 1 |
| | Soy milk | |

1. In a small skillet, heat oil over low heat. Add sausage, shallots, peas, carrots and sage; cook, stirring, for 15 minutes. Stir in soy cream, then season to taste with salt and pepper; cook, stirring, for 2 minutes.

2. Cut 8 large circles of pie dough and press into bottom and up sides of prepared muffin cups, reserving scraps. Fill with sausage mixture.

3. Form remaining dough scraps into a ball. Roll out dough, then cut into 8 small circles. Place one circle on top of each tart and seal edges. Brush dough with soy milk.

4. Bake in preheated oven for about 20 minutes or until tarts are golden brown.

# Classic Vegan Puff Pastry

You can make ready-made vegan puff pastry dough yourself, and I promise it's not as difficult as you might think.

## MAKES 1 LARGE SHEET OF PASTRY DOUGH (ABOUT 23 OZ/650 G)

| | | |
|---|---|---|
| 1¾ cup + 5 tsp | all-purpose flour | 250 g |
| Pinch | salt | Pinch |
| ¾ cup + 5 tsp | cold water | 200 mL |
| ¾ cup + 2 tbsp | vegan margarine (such as Earth Balance buttery sticks), softened | 200 g |
| | Additional all-purpose flour | |

1. Sift flour and salt into a large bowl. Add cold water and mix to form a dough.

2. Knead dough on a floured work surface. Form dough into a ball and place on a large sheet of parchment paper. Using a rolling pin, flatten ball on four sides, leaving a thicker area in the middle. Press dough on each side to form a cross, maintaining the thicker area in the middle. Slightly flatten the middle part of the dough.

3. Flatten margarine between 2 sheets of parchment paper until it is the same thickness and size as the middle square of the dough cross. Place margarine in middle of cross and fold the four sides over it to form a square.

4. Roll the square out in one direction to stretch into a rectangle. Fold the top third toward the center, then fold up the bottom third, like folding a letter.

5. Sprinkle dough with flour if necessary to prevent sticking, then rotate the rectangle a quarter turn and repeat step 4. Refrigerate dough on parchment paper for 30 minutes.

6. Remove dough from refrigerator and repeat step 4 two more times, sprinkling with flour as necessary and rotating dough a quarter turn in between. Refrigerate for 30 minutes.

7. Remove dough from refrigerator and repeat step 4 two more times (for a total of six times), sprinkling with flour as necessary and rotating dough a quarter turn in between. Refrigerate for at least 30 minutes, then roll out dough to ready it for use.

# Gluten-Free Vegan Puff Pastry

Here's a recipe for puff pastry that is gluten-free and without any dubious additives. The dough is moister, which keeps it from crumbling too easily. It is more fragile than wheat flour dough and should be handled with more care. If the dough is too sticky, flour your work surfaces. The dough will hold together well as it bakes.

## MAKES 1 SHEET OF DOUGH (ABOUT 19 OZ/550 G)

| | | |
|---|---|---|
| ¾ cup + 4 tsp | glutinous rice flour | 100 g |
| ⅔ cup + 2 tsp | corn flour | 80 g |
| ⅓ cup | millet flour | 40 g |
| ¼ cup | chickpea flour | 30 g |
| ½ tsp | xanthan gum | 1 g |
| Pinch | salt | Pinch |
| ⅔ cup | cold water | 150 mL |
| ¾ cup | vegan margarine | 175 g |
| | Additional glutinous rice flour | |

1. In a large bowl, combine flours, xanthan gum and salt. Add cold water and mix to form a dough.

2. Knead dough on a floured work surface. Form dough into a ball and place on a large sheet of parchment paper. Using a rolling pin, flatten ball on four sides, leaving a thicker area in the middle. Press dough on each side to form a cross, maintaining the thicker area in the middle. Slightly flatten the middle part of the dough.

3. Flatten margarine between 2 sheets of parchment paper until it is the same thickness and size as the middle square of the dough cross. Place margarine in middle of cross and fold the four sides over it to form a square.

4. Roll the square out in one direction to stretch into a rectangle. Fold the top third toward the center, then fold up the bottom third, like folding a letter.

5. Sprinkle dough with flour if necessary to prevent sticking, then rotate the rectangle a quarter turn and repeat step 4. Refrigerate dough on parchment paper for 30 minutes.

6. Remove dough from refrigerator and repeat step 4 two more times, sprinkling with flour as necessary and rotating dough a quarter turn in between. Refrigerate for 30 minutes.

7. Remove dough from refrigerator and repeat step 4 two more times (for a total of six times), sprinkling with flour as necessary and rotating dough a quarter turn in between. Refrigerate for at least 30 minutes, then roll out dough to ready it for use.

# Chestnut Vol-au-Vents

Here's a contemporary vegan version of vol-au-vents, starring chestnuts and smoked tofu. These can also be served with a salad for a light meal, or with a mushroom or white wine sauce as a more elaborate first course.

---

## MAKES 12 VOL-AU-VENTS

- Preheat oven to 350°F (180°C)
- 3-inch (7.5 cm) cookie cutter
- Smaller cookie cutter
- Large baking sheet, lined with parchment paper

| | | |
|---|---|---|
| 2 | sheets Classic Vegan Puff Pastry (page 40) | 2 |
| | Plain soy milk or other nondairy milk | |
| 1 tbsp | olive oil | 15 mL |
| 2 | shallots, minced | 2 |
| 2 | cloves garlic, minced | 2 |
| 7 oz | plain cooked chestnuts, chopped | 200 g |
| 3½ oz | firm smoked tofu, crumbled | 100 g |
| 1 tbsp | finely chopped dried porcini mushrooms | 2.25 g |
| 1 tbsp | chopped fresh chives | 3 g |
| ⅓ cup | soy cream | 75 mL |
| | Salt and freshly ground black pepper | |

## TIP

Look for cooked peeled chestnuts in packages, often shelved in the produce section or in jars in the imported foods section of well-stocked supermarkets and gourmet specialty stores.

1. Use the 3-inch (7.5 cm) cookie cutter to cut 12 circles from 1 sheet of puff pastry.

2. Using the smaller cookie cutter, cut out a circle in the middle of 6 of the larger circles, then lift out the smaller circles to leave rings (reserve the smaller circles). Place rings on the remaining 6 larger circles. Use a knife to cut notches around the ring while pressing the ring into the base to seal. Use a knife to cut slashes across the small circles of dough.

3. Repeat steps 1 and 2 with the second sheet of puff pastry to obtain 12 vol-au-vents. Place the stacked vol-au-vents and the 12 smaller circles on prepared baking sheet and brush with soy milk.

4. Bake in preheated oven for 15 minutes or until pastry is golden brown.

5. In a skillet, heat oil over high heat. Sauté shallots and garlic until fragrant. Add chestnuts and tofu; cook, stirring, for 3 minutes. Add mushrooms, chives, soy cream and salt and pepper to taste; cook, stirring, for 2 to 3 minutes.

6. Fill pastry shells with chestnut filling, then top each with a small circle of pastry crust. Serve hot.

# Cream of Leek Turnovers

These irresistible little turnovers are crisp on the outside, with a delicate cheesy filling that melts in your mouth. My advice: keep some set aside, or they'll disappear before you know it!

◆

## MAKES ABOUT 20 TURNOVERS

- Preheat oven to 350°F (180°C)
- 3-inch (7.5 cm) cookie cutter
- Large baking sheet, lined with parchment paper

| | | |
|---|---|---|
| 1 tbsp | olive oil | 15 mL |
| 8 oz | leeks (white and light green parts only), thinly sliced | 250 g |
| 2 | shallots, finely chopped | 2 |
| 2 | cloves garlic, minced | 2 |
| | Salt and freshly ground black pepper | |
| 3 tbsp | water | 45 mL |
| 2 tbsp | white wine | 30 mL |
| 1 tbsp | nutritional yeast | 4 g |
| 1 tsp | raw cane sugar | 4 g |
| ½ tsp | ground coriander | 1 g |
| ⅔ cup | soy cream | 150 mL |
| 1 tbsp | white miso | 15 mL |
| 2 | sheets Classic Vegan Puff Pastry (page 40) | 2 |
| | Plain soy or other nondairy milk | |
| 1 tbsp | poppy seeds | 9 g |

1. In a large skillet, heat oil over medium heat. Add leeks, shallots and garlic; cook, stirring, for 5 minutes or until browned. Season to taste with salt and pepper. Add water and cook for 5 minutes. Add wine and cook, scraping up any brown bits from the bottom of the pan, for 1 minute. Add yeast, sugar, coriander, soy cream and miso, stirring until well combined and heated through. Remove from heat.

2. Using the cookie cutter, cut out about 10 circles from each sheet of puff pastry. Place 1 tsp (5 mL) leek mixture in the center of each circle, fold dough over into a half-moon and seal edges with a fork. Place turnovers on prepared baking sheet, brush with soy milk and sprinkle poppy seeds on top.

3. Bake in preheated oven for 12 to 15 minutes or until turnovers are golden brown.

# Puff Pastry Stars

## with Chestnut and Sweet Potato Filling

Festive, pretty and easy to make, these pastry stars have it all! The delicately spiced filling will delight your guests.

◆

### MAKES ABOUT 20 PUFF PASTRIES

- Preheat oven to 300°F (150°C)
- 3-inch (7.5 cm) star-shaped cookie cutter
- Large baking sheet, lined with parchment paper

| | | |
|---|---|---|
| 1½ tbsp | olive oil or neutral vegetable oil | 22 mL |
| 7½ oz | sweet potato, peeled and cut into small cubes | 225 g |
| 4 oz | plain cooked chestnuts, crumbled | 125 g |
| 2 | cloves garlic, minced | 2 |
| 1 | small onion, minced | 1 |
| ¼ tsp | gingerbread spice | 0.5 g |
| Pinch | freshly ground black pepper | Pinch |
| ⅛ tsp | ground nutmeg | 0.5 g |
| ¾ cup + 5 tsp | water | 200 mL |
| ¼ cup | soy cream | 60 mL |
| 1 tbsp | tamari | 15 mL |
| 1 tbsp | white wine (optional) | 15 mL |
| 3 | sheets Classic Vegan Puff Pastry (page 40) | 3 |
| | Plain soy or other nondairy milk | |

1. In a large skillet, heat oil over high heat. Add sweet potato, chestnuts, garlic, onion, gingerbread spice, pepper and nutmeg; cook, stirring, for 5 minutes. Add water, reduce heat to medium and cook, stirring often, for 10 minutes. Stir in soy cream, tamari and wine (if using); cook for 2 minutes. Remove from heat and let cool.

2. Using the cookie cutter, cut out about 40 stars from puff pastry. Spoon filling into center of half the stars, place another star on top of each and use a fork to press down the edges to seal. Place filled stars on prepared baking sheet and brush with soy milk.

3. Bake in preheated oven for 10 to 15 minutes or until pastry is golden brown. Serve hot.

### TIP

Look for cooked peeled chestnuts in packages, often shelved in the produce section or in jars in the imported foods section of well-stocked supermarkets and gourmet specialty stores.

# Festive Party Dishes

## SOUPS

Shiitake Mushroom and
White Bean Soup
**50**

Winter Bisque
**53**

Ravioli in Flavored Broth
**54**

## MAIN DISHES

Holiday Roast
**57**

Lentil Wellington with
Roasted Carrots
**58**

Seitan Wellington
**61**

Tofu Medallions with Duxelles
and Squash
**62**

Swedish Meatballs with
Mustard Dill Sauce
**65**

Chestnut, Mushroom and
Hazelnut Paupiettes
**66**

Fisherman's Puff Pastries
**69**

Seitan Pot Pies
**70**

Sweet Potatoes Stuffed with
Chestnuts and Smoked Tempeh
**73**

Butternut Squash, Kale and
Ricotta Cannelloni
**74**

Mushroom and Walnut Ravioli
**77**

Porcini Mushroom Risotto
**78**

## SIDE DISHES

Roasted Beets and Onions
with Horseradish Dill Sauce
**81**

Mushroom Vegetable Crumble
**82**

Pommes Duchesse
**85**

Hasselback Potatoes with
Homemade Sage Butter
**86**

Herbed Potato Waffles
**89**

Potato Kohlrabi Pancakes
**90**

# Shiitake Mushroom and White Bean Soup

Smooth, silky and full-bodied thanks to the white beans, this vegan soup based on classic French velouté sauce proves that cream is far from essential in vegan cooking. This soup can be easily modified to suit your tastes, using squash, Jerusalem artichokes or other mushrooms.

◆

## MAKES 6 TO 8 SERVINGS

- Immersion blender (see tip)

| | | |
|---|---|---|
| ¼ cup | neutral vegetable oil | 60 mL |
| 7 oz | shiitake mushrooms, finely chopped | 200 g |
| 2 | large onions, finely chopped | 2 |
| 2 | cloves garlic, finely chopped | 2 |
| 2 tbsp | tamari | 30 mL |
| 1⅓ cups | drained cooked white beans | 250 g |
| 4¾ cups | water, divided (approx.) | 1.2 L |
| 3 tbsp | white miso | 45 mL |
| 2 tbsp | cashew butter | 30 mL |

## TIPS

If you don't have an immersion blender, you can transfer the soup to a regular blender, in batches as necessary, blend until smooth and then return to the pot to reheat.

Add some color and texture with toasted croutons and finely chopped chives.

1. In a large saucepan, heat oil over medium heat. Add mushrooms and onions; cook, stirring, for 10 minutes. Add garlic and tamari; cook, stirring, for 2 minutes.

2. Stir in beans, 3½ cups (875 mL) water and miso; reduce heat to low and simmer for 20 minutes. Stir in cashew butter and the remaining water. Remove from heat.

3. Using the immersion blender in the pot, blend to a smooth and even consistency, adding a little more water if desired if soup is too thick. Serve hot.

# Winter Bisque

Much more than a simple soup, this vegan bisque made with seasonal vegetables will delight your guests with its combination of subtle and pronounced flavors.

◆

## MAKES 8 SERVINGS

- Immersion blender (see tip, page 50)

| | | |
|---|---|---|
| 6 tbsp | olive oil, divided | 90 mL |
| 7 oz | mushrooms, diced | 200 g |
| 2 cups | diced peeled butternut squash | 300 g |
| 2 | medium potatoes, peeled and diced | 2 |
| 5 | cloves garlic, minced | 5 |
| 2 | onions, finely chopped | 2 |
| 2/3 cup | dry white wine | 150 mL |
| 1 2/3 cups | canned whole tomatoes, with juice | 400 g |
| 3 to 4 tbsp | flaked seaweed seasoning | 4.5 to 6 g |
| 4 3/4 cups | hot water (approx.) | 1.2 L |
| 3 tbsp | white miso | 45 mL |
| 1 tbsp | barley miso | 15 mL |
| 1/4 cup | tomato paste | 60 mL |
| 1 cup + 6 tbsp | soy cream | 350 mL |
| 1 1/2 tbsp | freshly squeezed lemon juice | 22 mL |
| | Salt, freshly ground black pepper and espelette pepper | |

## TIPS

If you can find Potimarron squash, a French heirloom variety of winter squash (also called Hokkaido or Kuri), it would be wonderful in this recipe.

Look for espelette pepper in the spice aisle of well-stocked grocery stores. It is often labeled Piment d'Espelette.

Try this winter bisque sprinkled with chopped parsley, seasoned soy cream and croutons.

1. In a skillet, heat 2 tbsp (30 mL) oil over medium heat. Add mushrooms and cook, stirring, for 5 to 10 minutes.

2. In a large pot, heat the remaining oil over medium heat. Add squash and potatoes; cook, stirring, for a few minutes. Stir in garlic and onions, then white wine, and cook, stirring, for 2 to 3 minutes.

3. Cut tomatoes into large pieces and add to the pot, along with their juice. Add seaweed seasoning and cook, stirring, for a few minutes. Add sautéed mushrooms.

4. Pour in a little of the hot water and stir in white miso, barley miso and tomato paste. Add the remaining water, reduce heat to medium-low and cook for 45 minutes or until vegetables are very soft.

5. Using the immersion blender in the pot, blend soup. Stir in soy cream, then lemon juice; thin with more water if soup is too thick. Season to taste with salt, black pepper and espelette pepper.

# Ravioli in Flavored Broth

This delicate and divine dish is an elegant alternative to the typical soup. As a bonus, it's a simple recipe for homemade ravioli that you can make year-round.

## MAKES 4 SERVINGS

- Food processor

### Ravioli Dough

| | | |
|---|---|---|
| 1½ cups | all-purpose flour | 200 g |
| Pinch | salt | Pinch |
| 7 tbsp + 1 tsp | hot water | 110 mL |
| ¾ cup | cornstarch (approx.) | 100 g |

### Broth

| | | |
|---|---|---|
| 1 tbsp | sesame oil | 15 mL |
| 1 | carrot, finely chopped | 1 |
| 1 | onion, finely chopped | 1 |
| ½ | leek (dark green part), finely chopped | ½ |
| 2 | cloves garlic, minced | 2 |
| 5 tsp | chopped gingerroot | 10 g |
| 1 tsp | Chinese five-spice powder | 2 g |
| 6 cups | hot water | 1.5 L |
| ¼ cup | tamari | 60 mL |
| 2 tbsp | white miso | 30 mL |

### Filling

| | | |
|---|---|---|
| 1 tbsp | olive oil or neutral vegetable oil | 15 mL |
| 1 | small carrot, finely diced | 1 |
| ½ | leek (white and light green part only), finely diced | ½ |
| 2 | shallots, finely chopped | 2 |
| 2 | cloves garlic, finely chopped | 2 |
| 3½ oz | smoked tempeh | 100 g |
| ½ tsp | ground coriander | 1 g |
| Pinch | freshly ground black pepper | Pinch |
| 2 tbsp | chopped chives | 6 g |
| 3 tbsp + 1 tsp | white wine | 50 mL |

1. *Dough:* In a round-bottomed mixing bowl, combine flour and salt. Add hot water and mix together. Knead until you have a ball of dough that is supple and very consistent in texture. Wrap dough in plastic wrap and refrigerate for 30 minutes.

2. *Broth:* In a large saucepan, heat sesame oil over medium heat. Add carrot, onion and leek; cook, stirring, for 2 minutes. Stir in garlic, ginger, five-spice powder, hot water, tamari and miso; cook, stirring occasionally, for 30 minutes. Strain out solids, set broth aside and keep hot.

3. *Filling:* In a medium skillet, heat oil over high heat. Add carrot and leek; cook, stirring, for 3 minutes. Add shallots, garlic, tempeh, coriander and pepper; cook, stirring, for 1 minute. Reduce heat to medium and cook, stirring, for 4 minutes. Add chives and wine; reduce heat to low and cook for 10 minutes. Remove from heat and let cool slightly.

4. Transfer filling to food processor and process to a very fine texture.

5. Roll a small piece of dough into a ball, flatten it and sprinkle it with cornstarch. On a work surface sprinkled with cornstarch, roll out the flattened ball into a thin circle. Spoon filling onto ravioli, moisten edges with water, then fold ravioli into a half-moon shape and pinch to seal edges. Repeat until all of the dough and filling are used.

6. In a large pot of boiling water, cook ravioli for 4 minutes. Transfer ravioli to soup plates and pour broth over top, dividing evenly.

### TIP

Serve with lemon wedges on the side for squeezing, and save some finely diced leek for garnish.

# Holiday Roast

Although you can find tofu-based vegan alternatives to turkey with stuffing (including the famous Tofurky brand) in grocery stores, with a little patience and some precision, you can make your own roast tofu with stuffing.

## MAKES 10 TO 12 SERVINGS

- Preheat oven to 350°F (180°C)
- Fine-mesh sieve, lined with cheesecloth
- Large baking sheet, lined with foil
- Kitchen string

### Tofu Layer

| | | |
|---|---|---|
| 1¾ lbs | firm tofu, crumbled | 800 g |
| 1 tbsp | vegetable bouillon powder | 6 g |
| 1 tsp | garlic powder | 3 g |
| 1 tsp | ground paprika | 2 g |
| 1 tsp | dried oregano | 1 g |
| 1 tsp | dried thyme | 1 g |
| ½ tsp | dried rosemary | 0.5 g |
| ½ tsp | freshly ground black pepper | 1 g |

### Stuffing

| | | |
|---|---|---|
| 2 tbsp | olive oil or neutral vegetable oil | 30 mL |
| 3 | apples, diced | 3 |
| 2 | cloves garlic, minced | 2 |
| 1 | onion, finely chopped | 1 |
| 10 | fresh sage leaves, chopped | 10 |
| | Large handful walnuts, chopped | |
| ¾ cup | crushed rusks | 80 g |
| ¾ cup + 5 tsp | ready-to-use vegetable broth | 200 mL |
| 1 tbsp | tamari | 15 mL |

### Glaze

| | | |
|---|---|---|
| 2 tbsp | sesame oil | 30 mL |
| 2 tbsp | white miso | 30 mL |
| 1 tbsp | tamari | 15 mL |
| 1 tbsp | water | 15 mL |
| 1 tsp | smoked paprika | 2 g |

1. *Tofu Layer:* Place tofu in lined sieve. Place sieve on a soup dish and place a fairly heavy weight on top to press tofu. Let drain in refrigerator for 2 hours.

2. In a bowl, combine drained tofu, bouillon powder, garlic powder, paprika, oregano, thyme, rosemary and pepper.

3. *Stuffing:* In a large skillet, heat oil over high heat. Add apples, garlic and onion; cook, stirring, until starting to brown. Reduce heat to medium and stir in sage, walnuts, rusks and broth; cook for 5 minutes or until apples are softened. Remove from heat and stir in tamari.

4. Place 2 large sheets of parchment paper crosswise on prepared baking sheet. Spread two-thirds of the tofu mixture in the center, in an area measuring about 12 by 4 inches (30 by 10 cm). Press down firmly in the center to form a compact layer.

5. Place stuffing in center of tofu layer, packing it down firmly. Pack edges of tofu layer around stuffing. Add the remaining tofu mixture on top. Pack tofu with your hands to shape the roast. There should not be any holes in the tofu layer, and it should be uniform in thickness (about ½ inch/1 cm thick) around the entire roast.

6. Fold over the sheets of parchment paper to help shape the roast, just tightly enough to give it a cylindrical shape. This step is the most delicate one. Don't hesitate to start over a few times until you have shaped the roast correctly. Warning: If the parchment paper gets too damp, it can tear, so don't stretch it too much. Once the roast is rolled in the parchment paper, tie it up with string, not too tightly, and close up both ends. Fold foil around parchment paper.

7. Bake in preheated oven for 45 minutes.

8. *Glaze:* In a small bowl, combine sesame oil, miso, tamari, water and paprika.

9. Unwrap roast and place on a baking sheet. Brush with glaze and bake for 5 minutes. Brush with glaze again and bake for 10 minutes.

# Lentil Wellington
## with Roasted Carrots

Here's a vegan variation on the famous dish made of beef in puff pastry. This Wellington features simple ingredients — lentils, red kidney beans and carrots — for comfort food everyone will love. Serve with mashed sweet potatoes.

✦

## MAKES 8 SERVINGS

- Preheat oven to 350°F (180°C)
- 2 baking sheets, lined with parchment paper

### Lentil Filling

| | | |
|---|---|---|
| 2 tbsp | olive oil | 30 mL |
| 2 | onions, finely chopped | 2 |
| 3 | cloves garlic, minced | 3 |
| ¾ cup + 2 tbsp | drained cooked red kidney beans, mashed | 150 g |
| 1½ cups | drained cooked lentils | 300 g |
| ½ | beet, finely shredded into a purée (see tip) | ½ |
| ¾ cup | mashed cooked potatoes | 150 g |
| 1 tbsp | chopped fresh thyme | 3 g |
| 1 tbsp | chopped fresh parsley | 4 g |
| 5 | fresh sage leaves, finely chopped | 5 |
| 2 tbsp | barley miso | 30 mL |

### Roasted Carrots

| | | |
|---|---|---|
| 10 oz | carrots, peeled and cut into sticks | 300 g |
| 1 tbsp | olive oil | 15 mL |
| 1 tbsp | chopped fresh thyme | 3 g |
| | Salt and freshly ground black pepper | |
| 1 | sheet Classic Vegan Puff Pastry (page 40) | 1 |
| | Duxelles (see Tofu Medallions with Duxelles and Squash, page 62) | |
| | Plain soy or other nondairy milk | |

## TIPS

Use a fine grater to shred beets into a purée.

In place of the carrots, you can use another vegetable, such as parsnips or squash.

1. *Filling:* In a skillet, heat oil over medium heat. Add onions and cook, stirring, until softened. Add garlic, beans and lentils; cook, stirring, until garlic is fragrant. Add beet purée, mashed potatoes, thyme, parsley, sage and miso, stirring well. Cook for 6 to 7 minutes, mashing until filling is smooth.

2. *Carrots:* In a large bowl, toss carrots with oil, thyme and salt and pepper to taste. Spread out in a single layer on a prepared baking sheet. Bake in preheated oven until golden and soft (baking time depends on the size of the sticks). Remove from oven, leaving oven on.

3. Lay puff pastry on the other prepared baking sheet. Spread duxelles on top, leaving a ½- to 1-inch (1 to 2.5 cm) border of plain dough. Spread two-thirds of the filling in the center, in a strip measuring about 10 by 4 inches (25 by 10 cm). Lay roasted carrots on top of filling, then cover with the remaining filling. Using your hands, press filling into a rounded loaf. Gently fold puff pastry dough over filling to completely seal it in.

4. Gently turn the Wellington so it is seal side down. This step is the most delicate. Use parchment paper to turn it over onto another sheet of parchment paper if needed, or use spatulas. Be careful not to tear the puff pastry. With the back of a knife, score lines in the dough, then brush dough with milk.

5. Bake for 35 to 40 minutes or until pastry is golden brown.

# Seitan Wellington

Here's another vegan version of beef Wellington, made with homemade seitan.
It's a slightly more complicated recipe than the Lentil Wellington (page 58),
but the results are impressive. Serve with herb-roasted potatoes and gravy.

## MAKES 8 SERVINGS

- Cheesecloth and kitchen string (optional)
- Baking sheet, lined with parchment paper

### Broth

| | | |
|---|---|---|
| 2 tbsp | minced garlic | 30 g |
| 1 tbsp | chopped fresh thyme | 3 g |
| 1 tsp | smoked paprika | 2 g |
| 1/2 tsp | freshly ground black pepper | 1 g |
| 1/4 cup | barley miso | 60 mL |
| 2 tbsp | tamari | 30 mL |
| 1 tbsp | prepared mustard | 15 mL |
| 8 cups | boiling water | 2 L |

### Seitan

| | | |
|---|---|---|
| 2 cups | vital wheat gluten (approx.) | 250 g |
| 2/3 cup + 2 tsp | chickpea flour | 85 g |
| 1/2 tsp | garlic powder | 1 g |
| 1/2 tsp | ground coriander | 1 g |
| 2 tbsp | toasted sesame oil | 30 mL |
| 1 tbsp | tomato paste | 15 mL |

### Chestnut Duxelles

| | | |
|---|---|---|
| 1 tsp | olive oil | 5 mL |
| 12 oz | mushrooms, finely chopped | 350 g |
| 3 1/2 oz | peeled cooked chestnuts, finely chopped | 100 g |
| 1 | sheet Classic Vegan Puff Pastry (page 40) | 1 |
| | Plain soy or other nondairy milk | |

### TIP

Prepare the seitan and duxelles the day before. Store the duxelles in an airtight container and the seitan immersed in broth in the refrigerator. The Wellington will taste even better, and you'll only need to assemble it and pop it in the oven the next day.

1. *Broth:* In a large pot, combine garlic, thyme, paprika, pepper, miso, tamari and mustard. Thin with a little boiling water, then pour in the remaining water, stirring well. Remove 1 cup (250 mL) broth and strain it into a bowl. Keep the remaining broth hot over low heat.

2. *Seitan:* In a bowl, combine wheat gluten and chickpea flour.

3. To the bowl of strained broth, add garlic powder, coriander, sesame oil and tomato paste. Pour over flour mixture and stir with a spatula to form mixture into a ball. Add a little more wheat gluten if the mixture seems very sticky.

4. On a floured work surface, knead seitan, then form into a cylinder slightly shorter than the length of the puff pastry. (For a firmer, rounder seitan, wrap the cylinder in a sheet of cheesecloth and tie it with string.) Place seitan in pot of broth, adding hot water if necessary to immerse. Cook over medium heat for 30 minutes.

5. *Duxelles:* Meanwhile, in a large skillet, heat oil over medium heat. Add mushrooms and chestnuts; cook, stirring often, for 10 minutes.

6. Preheat oven to 350°F (180°C).

7. Thoroughly drain cooked seitan. Lay puff pastry on prepared baking sheet. Spread duxelles evenly over pastry, leaving a 1/2- to 1-inch (1 to 2.5 cm) border of plain dough. Lay seitan on dough, then roll dough around it. Cut off excess dough if necessary and seal seitan airtight. Gently turn the Wellington so it is seal side down. With the back of a knife, score lines or a grid in the dough, then brush dough with milk.

8. Bake for 25 minutes or until pastry is golden brown.

# Tofu Medallions

## with Duxelles and Squash

This simple but intensely flavored dish raises tofu to new heights and highlights seasonal foods. It's perfect if you don't like making large quantities or if you're looking for ideas for a meal to serve the day after a holiday feast.

◆

## MAKES 4 SERVINGS

- 2¾-inch (7 cm) round cookie cutter

### Duxelles

| | | |
|---|---|---|
| 1 tbsp | neutral vegetable oil | 15 mL |
| 10 oz | mushrooms, peeled and finely chopped | 300 g |
| 2 | large shallots, finely chopped | 2 |
| | Salt and freshly ground black pepper | |

### Squash

| | | |
|---|---|---|
| 2 tbsp | neutral vegetable oil | 30 mL |
| 1 lb | butternut squash or pie pumpkin, peeled and cut into medium cubes | 500 g |
| | Salt and freshly ground black pepper | |
| | Handful of hazelnuts, chopped | |

### Tofu Medallions

| | | |
|---|---|---|
| 14 oz | firm tofu | 400 g |
| 2 tbsp | toasted sesame oil | 30 mL |
| 1 tsp | Chinese five-spice powder | 2 g |
| Pinch | freshly ground black pepper | Pinch |
| 1 tbsp | tamari | 15 mL |

### Sauce

| | | |
|---|---|---|
| 1 cup | soy cream | 250 mL |
| ¼ cup | dry white wine | 60 mL |
| 2 tbsp | white miso | 30 mL |

## TIP

If you can find Potimarron squash, a French heirloom variety of winter squash (also called Hokkaido or Kuri), it would be wonderful in this recipe.

1. *Duxelles:* In a medium skillet, heat oil over medium heat. Add mushrooms and shallots; cook, stirring often, for 10 minutes. Season to taste with salt and pepper. Remove from heat.

2. *Squash:* In a large skillet, heat oil over high heat. Add squash and cook, stirring, for 5 minutes. Reduce heat to medium and cook, stirring often, for 15 minutes. Season to taste with salt and pepper and stir in hazelnuts.

3. *Tofu Medallions:* Meanwhile, cut tofu into 4 slices. Using the cookie cutter, cut tofu slices into medallions. In another large skillet, heat sesame oil, five-spice powder and pepper over high heat. Add tofu and cook until browned on both sides. Remove from heat, add tamari and let caramelize for 30 seconds per side.

4. *Sauce:* In a small saucepan over low heat, whisk together soy cream, wine and miso until well combined and flavors are blended.

5. Serve tofu medallions with sauce, duxelles and squash.

# Swedish Meatballs

## with Mustard Dill Sauce

This rustic holiday meal features a vegan version of the famous Swedish meatballs, with a creamy dill sauce. Serve with tart lingonberries, comforting potato purée and a small salad for extra color.

◆

## MAKES 6 TO 8 SERVINGS

### Broth

| | | |
|---|---|---|
| 2 cups | boiling water | 500 mL |
| 2 tbsp | soy sauce | 30 mL |
| 1 tbsp | barley miso | 15 mL |
| 1 tbsp | tomato paste | 15 mL |
| ½ tsp | garlic powder | 1 g |
| ½ tsp | liquid smoke | 2 mL |
| | Freshly ground black pepper | |

### Vegan Meatballs

| | | |
|---|---|---|
| 5 oz | textured vegetable protein (TVP) | 150 g |
| 1 cup | dry bread crumbs | 100 g |
| 1 tsp | garlic powder | 3 g |
| ½ tsp | ground allspice | 1 g |
| 1 tbsp | olive oil | 15 mL |
| 1 | large onion, finely chopped | 1 |
| 3 tbsp | finely chopped fresh parsley | 12 g |
| 6½ tbsp | chickpea flour | 50 g |
| 1 cup | plain soy milk | 250 mL |
| | Salt and freshly ground black pepper | |
| | Neutral vegetable oil | |

### Mustard Dill Sauce

| | | |
|---|---|---|
| 2 cups | soy cream | 500 mL |
| 1 tbsp | old-fashioned (grainy) mustard | 15 mL |
| 1 tbsp | Dijon mustard | 15 mL |
| 1 tbsp | raw cane sugar | 12 g |
| 2 tsp | chopped fresh dill | 2 g |
| | Salt and freshly ground black pepper | |

1. *Broth:* In a large bowl, combine boiling water, soy sauce, miso, tomato paste, garlic powder, liquid smoke and pepper to taste.

2. *Meatballs:* Add vegetable protein to broth and rehydrate for 30 minutes. Drain to remove excess liquid, if necessary (the vegetable protein will absorb the broth). Transfer to another bowl and incorporate bread crumbs, garlic powder and allspice.

3. In a skillet, heat olive oil over medium heat. Add onion and cook, stirring, until softened, then stir in parsley.

4. Add onion mixture to vegetable protein mixture, mixing well. Add chickpea flour and soy milk. Season with salt and pepper, mix well, then let set for 10 minutes. Using your hands, form mixture into meatballs.

5. In a clean skillet, heat vegetable oil over medium heat. Cook meatballs, turning often, for 5 minutes.

6. *Sauce:* In a small saucepan over low heat, combine soy cream, old-fashioned mustard, Dijon mustard, sugar and dill. Season to taste with salt and pepper. Cook, stirring often, for 5 minutes.

## TIPS

If you prefer, you can bake the meatballs instead of frying them. Place lightly oiled meatballs on a baking sheet lined with parchment paper and bake in a preheated 350°F (180°C) oven for 10 to 15 minutes.

The meatballs can be made ahead and reheated in the skillet or oven, but the sauce must be made just before serving.

# Chestnut, Mushroom and Hazelnut Paupiettes

These beautifully browned nuggets with a tender filling will add a traditional touch to your holiday meal, but can also grace the dinner table year-round with seasonal ingredients in the filling. Serve with baby green peas and a gravy-like brown sauce (or your choice of sauce).

## MAKES 8 SERVINGS

- Kitchen string
- Steamer basket
- Baking dish

### Filling

| | | |
|---|---|---|
| 2 tbsp | olive oil | 30 mL |
| 6 oz | mushrooms, peeled | 170 g |
| 3 | shallots, finely chopped | 3 |
| 3 | cloves garlic, minced | 3 |
| 6 tbsp + 2 tsp | dry white wine | 100 mL |
| 10 oz | peeled cooked chestnuts, crumbled or crushed with a fork | 300 g |
| 9 tbsp | crushed hazelnuts | 75 g |
| 1 tbsp | chopped fresh parsley | 4 g |
| 1 tbsp | tamari | 15 mL |

### Seitan

| | | |
|---|---|---|
| 2½ cups | vital wheat gluten | 300 g |
| ⅔ cup + 2 tsp | corn flour | 80 g |
| 2 tsp | garlic powder | 6 g |
| ½ tsp | smoked paprika | 1 g |
| ½ tsp | ground coriander | 1 g |
| ¼ tsp | ground cumin | 0.5 g |
| ½ | cube vegetable bouillon | ½ |
| 2 cups | warm water | 500 mL |
| ¼ cup | tamari | 60 mL |
| 2 tbsp | white miso | 30 mL |
| | Glaze (see Holiday Roast, page 57) | |

1. *Filling:* In a large skillet, heat oil over high heat. Add mushrooms, shallots and garlic; cook, stirring, for 3 minutes. Reduce heat to medium and cook, stirring, for 5 minutes. Add wine and cook until evaporated. Add chestnuts and hazelnuts; cook, stirring, for 3 minutes. Add parsley and tamari; cook, stirring, for 2 minutes. Remove from heat.

2. *Seitan:* In a large bowl, combine wheat gluten, corn flour, garlic powder, paprika, coriander and cumin.

3. In another bowl, combine bouillon cube, warm water, tamari and miso. Pour over dry ingredients and stir vigorously.

4. Remove seitan from bowl and knead on a work surface for a few minutes. Separate seitan into 4 or 8 balls (larger balls are easier to shape). Flatten each ball, add filling on top, then roll into a cylinder, pinching ends to enclose filling. Wrap each paupiette in parchment paper and tie with string (not too tightly, as paupiettes will expand a little while cooking).

5. In a steamer basket set over a large pot of boiling water, steam paupiettes for 30 to 40 minutes, depending on whether you have made 8 small or 4 large paupiettes.

6. Meanwhile, preheat oven to 350°F (180°C).

7. Unwrap paupiettes, place in a baking dish and brush with glaze.

8. Bake for 5 minutes. If you have opted for 4 large paupiettes, cut them in half when ready to serve.

# Fisherman's Puff Pastries

The flavors of the sea are usually forgotten when it comes to vegan holiday recipes. That's a shame, because with just a few ingredients, we can reproduce tastes and textures that will surprise and delight the most skeptical dinner guests. These puff pastries are a wonderful example.

## MAKES 4 TO 8 SERVINGS

- Preheat oven to 325°F (160°C)
- Large baking sheet, lined with parchment paper

| | | |
|---|---|---|
| 2 tbsp | olive oil or neutral vegetable oil | 30 mL |
| 1 | large onion, finely chopped | 1 |
| 1 cup | finely chopped fennel bulb | 100 g |
| 2 | cloves garlic, minced | 2 |
| 7 oz | soft smoked tofu, crumbled | 200 g |
| 2 tsp | chopped fresh dill (or 1 tsp/1 g dried dillweed) | 2 g |
| 2 tsp | chopped fresh chives | 2 g |
| 2 tsp | flaked seaweed seasoning | 1 g |
| Pinch | freshly ground black pepper | Pinch |
| 1 tbsp | freshly squeezed lemon juice | 15 mL |
| 3 tbsp | soy cream | 45 mL |
| 2 | sheets Classic Vegan Puff Pastry (page 40) | 2 |
| | Plain soy or other nondairy milk | |

1. In a large skillet, heat oil over medium-high heat. Add onion and fennel; cook, stirring, until softened. Reduce heat to medium. Stir in garlic and tofu; cook for 1 minute. Stir in dill, chives, seaweed seasoning, pepper and lemon juice; reduce heat to medium-low and cook for a few more minutes. Stir in soy cream and cook for 2 minutes. Remove from heat.

2. Cut 4 squares from each sheet of puff pastry and arrange on prepared baking sheet. Add filling to the center of each square, dividing evenly, then fold the corners of the squares toward the centers. Brush squares with milk.

3. Bake in preheated oven for 15 minutes or until pastry is golden brown.

# Seitan Pot Pies

These individual pot pies feature crisp, golden pastry covering a bed of tender vegetables, for a sophisticated but easy-to-serve dinner.

◆

## MAKES 6 POT PIES

- Preheat oven to 325°F (160°C)
- 6 large ramekins or individual baking dishes, lightly oiled

| | | |
|---|---|---|
| 2 tbsp | olive oil | 30 mL |
| 3 | cloves garlic, minced | 3 |
| 1 | red onion, finely chopped | 1 |
| 1 | shallot, minced | 1 |
| 8 oz | seitan, diced | 250 g |
| 10 oz | blanched artichoke bottoms or peeled Jerusalem artichokes, diced | 300 g |
| ½ tsp | dried thyme | 0.5 g |
| ¾ cup | ready-to-use vegetable broth | 175 mL |
| 2 tbsp | white wine | 30 mL |
| | Salt and freshly ground black pepper | |
| 1 | sheet Classic Vegan Puff Pastry (page 40) | 1 |
| | Plain soy or other nondairy milk | |

## TIP

These little pot pies go beautifully with roasted potatoes and a salad.

1. In a large skillet, heat oil over medium heat. Add garlic, onion and shallot; cook, stirring, until softened. Add seitan, artichokes and thyme; cook, stirring, for 10 minutes. Stir in broth and wine; increase heat to high and cook for 5 minutes or until vegetables are tender but still firm. Season to taste with salt and pepper.

2. Fill ramekins with seitan mixture. Cut out 6 pieces of puff pastry the same size as your ramekins and place pastry on top of ramekins. Brush pastry with milk.

3. Bake in preheated oven for 15 to 20 minutes or until crust is golden brown and crispy.

## VARIATIONS

The pot pies can also be made with a double crust. I suggest using prebaked short-crust pastry for the bottom crust before adding the filling and the puff pastry top crust.

You can also make one individual pie. Use a classic pie pan and pinch the edges of the pastry against the pan to seal.

Other vegetables, such as squash, mushrooms, celery root, parsnips or carrots, can be substituted for the artichokes.

# Sweet Potatoes

## Stuffed with Chestnuts and Smoked Tempeh

The sweetness of chestnuts and sweet potatoes contrasts with smoked tempeh and smooth herb cream in this delightful gourmet wintertime dish! Add a fresh, crisp touch with green vegetables or salad on the side.

◆

### MAKES 6 SERVINGS

- Baking dish

| | | |
|---|---|---|
| 6 | medium sweet potatoes | 6 |
| 2 tbsp | olive oil | 30 mL |
| 2 | shallots, finely chopped | 2 |
| 2 | cloves garlic, minced | 2 |
| 3½ oz | peeled cooked chestnuts, crumbled | 100 g |
| 3½ oz | smoked tempeh, crumbled | 100 g |
| 1 tbsp | chopped fresh parsley | 4 g |
| 1 tbsp | finely chopped fresh chives | 3 g |
| 1 tsp | dried thyme | 1 g |
| ⅔ cup | soy cream | 150 mL |
| | Salt and freshly ground black pepper | |
| 1 to 2 tbsp | nutritional yeast | 4 to 8 g |
| | Additional olive oil | |

1. Place sweet potatoes in a pot of cold water and bring to a boil. Boil for 25 minutes.

2. Meanwhile, in a large skillet, heat oil over medium heat. Add shallots and garlic; cook, stirring, for 1 minute. Add chestnuts and tempeh; cook, stirring, for 5 minutes. Add parsley, chives, thyme and soy cream. Season to taste with salt and pepper. Cook until texture is creamy.

3. Preheat oven to 350°F (180°C).

4. Place sweet potatoes in baking dish. Using a knife, trace an oval in each sweet potato, remove skin from oval and scoop out interior, leaving a little flesh so as not to pierce the skin. Stuff sweet potatoes with tempeh mixture and sprinkle with nutritional yeast. Lightly oil sweet potatoes.

5. Bake for 15 to 20 minutes.

# Butternut Squash, Kale and Ricotta Cannelloni

Holiday meals don't need to be decadent. The proof: kale, the star of healthy cuisine, is invited to the table in light cannelloni with vegan ricotta and butternut squash. A perfect day-after dish! Serve with a green salad for a light meal.

## MAKES 4 SERVINGS

- Preheat oven to 350°F (180°C)
- Baking dish

### Filling

| | | |
|---|---|---|
| 14 oz | firm tofu, crumbled | 400 g |
| ¾ cup | Homemade Vegan Crème Fraîche (page 27) or vegan sour cream | 200 g |
| 1 tsp | salt | 6 g |
| 2 tbsp | olive oil | 30 mL |
| 10 oz | butternut squash, peeled and finely diced | 300 g |
| 4 | shallots, minced | 4 |
| 2 | cloves garlic, minced | 2 |
| 3 cups | packed finely chopped trimmed kale leaves (tough stems and center ribs removed) | 100 g |
| | Salt and freshly ground black pepper | |

### Cannelloni

| | | |
|---|---|---|
| 16 | vegan cannelloni pasta tubes, cooked and drained (or fresh pasta sheets) | 16 |
| 4 cups | vegan béchamel | 1 L |
| | Nutritional yeast | |

1. *Filling:* In a bowl, combine tofu, crème fraîche and salt.

2. In a large skillet, heat oil over medium heat. Add squash, shallots, garlic and kale; cook, stirring, for 5 minutes. Add tofu mixture and season to taste with salt and pepper; cook for 1 minute.

3. *Cannelloni:* Stuff cannelloni tubes with filling (or spoon onto sheets and roll into cylinders). Pour a little béchamel into baking dish, then arrange cannelloni side by side in dish. Cover with the remaining béchamel and sprinkle nutritional yeast on top.

4. Bake in preheated oven for 25 minutes.

# Mushroom and Walnut Ravioli

If you need to come up with a last-minute dish that isn't too rich or tricky to make, this quick and easy ravioli fills the bill!

## MAKES 4 SERVINGS

- Baking sheet, lined with lightly floured parchment paper
- Immersion blender

### Ravioli

| | | |
|---|---|---|
| 2 tbsp | olive oil | 30 mL |
| 8 oz | mushrooms, finely diced | 250 g |
| 1/4 cup | chopped walnuts | 30 g |
| 2 tbsp | minced garlic | 30 g |
| 1 tsp | soy sauce | 5 mL |
| | Salt and freshly ground black pepper | |
| 24 | square wonton wrappers | 24 |

### Sauce

| | | |
|---|---|---|
| 1 tbsp | olive oil | 15 mL |
| 4 oz | mushrooms, finely chopped | 125 g |
| 2/3 cup | soy cream | 150 mL |
| 1 to 2 tbsp | white wine | 15 to 30 mL |
| | Salt and freshly ground black pepper | |

## TIP

Buy a few packages of wonton wrappers and freeze them. That way, you'll always have some on hand to make ravioli!

1. *Ravioli:* In a large skillet, heat oil over medium heat. Add mushrooms and cook, stirring often, for 5 minutes. Add walnuts, garlic and soy sauce; cook, stirring, for 5 minutes or until filling is very dry. Season to taste with salt and pepper.

2. Place 1 tsp (5 mL) filling in the center of a wonton wrapper. Using a brush dipped in water, lightly moisten edges of wonton wrapper. Fold over diagonally to form a triangle. Moisten two ends and fold one over the other. Repeat with the remaining filling and wonton wrappers. Arrange ravioli on prepared baking sheet, spacing them evenly.

3. *Sauce:* In a small saucepan, heat oil over medium heat. Add mushrooms and cook, stirring, for 5 minutes. Stir in soy cream and wine. Season to taste with salt and pepper. Using the immersion blender in the pan, blend sauce. Remove from heat and keep warm.

4. In a pot of boiling salted water, cook ravioli for 1 minute. Drain and serve immediately with sauce.

# Porcini Mushroom Risotto

This versatile dish fits easily in your holiday dinner as a first course, main course or side dish. But the rich and creamy risotto, with its enchanting scent of mushrooms, will continue to be a favorite all year round.

◆

## MAKES 4 TO 8 SERVINGS

### Mushrooms

| | | |
|---|---|---|
| 1 cup | finely chopped dried porcini mushrooms | 33 g |
| | Warm water | |
| 2 tbsp | olive oil | 30 mL |
| 3½ oz | button mushrooms, diced | 100 g |
| 1 tbsp | chopped fresh parsley | 4 g |
| ½ tsp | dried sage | 0.5 g |
| 2 tbsp | dry white wine | 30 mL |
| | Salt and freshly ground black pepper | |

### Risotto

| | | |
|---|---|---|
| 2 tbsp | olive oil | 30 mL |
| 1 lb | carnaroli, Arborio or other round-grain rice | 500 g |
| ¾ cup + 5 tsp | dry white wine | 200 mL |
| 5¼ cups | hot ready-to-use vegetable broth | 1.3 L |
| 1 tbsp | nutritional yeast | 4 g |
| 2 tbsp | vegan margarine | 28 g |
| 2 tbsp | cashew butter | 30 mL |

## TIPS

The best way to make sure your risotto is perfect is to stir constantly throughout the cooking process.

You can prepare the mushrooms ahead of time, but the risotto must be made just before serving and cannot be reheated (the rice will continue to cook and absorb liquid, which will make it pasty). To save time on the day of the meal, prepare all of your ingredients in advance.

1. *Mushrooms:* Rehydrate porcini mushrooms in a bowl of warm water for 20 minutes; drain well.

2. In a medium skillet, heat oil over medium heat. Add porcini and button mushrooms, parsley and sage; cook, stirring, for 10 minutes. Add wine, reduce heat to low and cook until wine is evaporated. Season to taste with salt and pepper. Remove from heat.

3. *Risotto:* In a large saucepan, heat oil over medium heat. Add rice and cook, stirring, until translucent and slightly pearly in color. Add wine and cook until completely absorbed. Add a ladleful of broth and stir until broth is absorbed. Continue stirring in broth, a ladleful at a time, until all of the broth is added and rice is creamy but firm, about 18 minutes.

4. Add mushrooms, stirring well. Remove from heat and stir in nutritional yeast, margarine and cashew butter. Serve immediately.

# Roasted Beets and Onions

## with Horseradish Dill Sauce

These delicious roasted root vegetables add color and zest to your holiday table. I like to serve them with a creamy horseradish dill sauce for a combination of flavors inspired by Slavic cuisine.

◆

## MAKES 6 SERVINGS

- Preheat oven to 350°F (180°C)
- Large baking dish

| | | |
|---|---|---|
| 4 | medium beets, cut into wedges of equal thickness | 4 |
| 4 | medium onions, cut into large wedges | 4 |
| | Olive oil | |
| | Salt and freshly ground black pepper | |

### Horseradish Dill Sauce

| | | |
|---|---|---|
| 7 oz | plain soy yogurt | 200 g |
| ¾ cup + 5 tsp | soy cream | 200 mL |
| 2 tbsp | freshly squeezed lemon juice | 30 mL |
| ½ to 2 tsp | horseradish (prepared, in a jar or in powder form) | 2 to 10 mL |
| 1 tsp | dried dillweed (or 2 tsp/2 g chopped fresh dill) | 1 g |
| | Salt and freshly ground black pepper | |

1. Place beets and onions in baking dish and drizzle with oil. Using your hands, mix vegetables until thoroughly coated in oil. Season lightly with salt and pepper. Bake in preheated oven for 30 minutes.

2. *Sauce:* In a small bowl, combine yogurt, soy cream, lemon juice, horseradish and dill. Season to taste with salt and pepper. Set aside in refrigerator.

3. Serve roasted beets and onions hot, drizzled with sauce.

# Mushroom Vegetable Crumble

This rustic gourmet dish is always a favorite. It's a perfect side dish for the holiday season, especially if you are not a seasoned chef.

## MAKES 4 TO 6 SERVINGS

- Preheat oven to 350°F (180°C)
- Baking sheet, lined with parchment paper
- 4 to 6 ramekins or individual small dishes

| | | |
|---|---|---|
| 1 tbsp | olive oil or neutral vegetable oil | 15 mL |
| 1 lb | button mushrooms, diced | 500 g |
| 2 | carrots, finely diced | 2 |
| 2 | small potatoes, peeled and finely diced | 2 |
| 2 | cloves garlic, minced | 2 |
| 6 tbsp + 2 tsp | dry white wine | 100 mL |
| 2 tbsp | finely chopped dried porcini mushrooms | 4.5 g |
| 5 | fresh sage leaves, chopped | 5 |
| 1¼ cups | soy cream | 300 mL |
| | Salt and freshly ground black pepper | |

## Crumble

| | | |
|---|---|---|
| 1 cup | whole wheat flour | 150 g |
| ½ cup | ground hazelnuts | 50 g |
| 1 tbsp | dried thyme | 3 g |
| Pinch | salt | Pinch |
| Pinch | freshly ground black pepper | Pinch |
| 3 tbsp | virgin coconut oil | 45 mL |

1. In a skillet, heat oil over medium heat. Add button mushrooms, carrots, potatoes and garlic; cook, stirring, for 5 minutes. Stir in wine. Add porcini mushrooms and sage; reduce heat to low and cook, stirring often, for 10 minutes. Add soy cream and season to taste with salt and pepper; cook, stirring, for 2 to 3 minutes.

2. *Crumble:* Meanwhile, in a round-bottomed bowl, using your hands, combine flour, hazelnuts, thyme, salt, pepper and coconut oil. Spread crumble on prepared baking sheet. Bake in preheated oven for 10 minutes.

3. Pour vegetable mixture into ramekins. Sprinkle with crumble and serve hot.

## TIP

Make the crumble while vegetables are cooking so that everything is ready at the same time.

# Pommes Duchesse

For a vegan version of this classic side dish, all you need to do is replace the butter and egg yolk with vegan ingredients. The result is just as gourmet and crispy-soft as the original.

## MAKES 4 TO 6 SERVINGS

- Preheat oven to 350°F (180°C)
- Pastry bag fitted with a large fluted piping tip
- Baking sheet, lined with parchment paper (or lightly oiled)

| | | |
|---|---|---|
| 1 lb 7 oz | potatoes, peeled | 650 g |
| ¼ cup | vegan margarine, cut into pieces | 60 g |
| 2 tbsp | cornstarch | 16 g |
| Pinch | ground turmeric | Pinch |
| 2 tbsp | cashew butter | 30 mL |
| 1 tbsp | neutral vegetable oil | 15 mL |
| | Additional vegan margarine, melted (optional) | |

1. Place potatoes in a pot of cold salted water and bring to a boil. Boil until fork-tender, then drain well. In pot, mash potatoes with margarine. Over low heat, thoroughly dry mashed potatoes for a few minutes.

2. In a small bowl, combine cornstarch, turmeric, cashew butter and oil. Using a spatula, incorporate mixture into mashed potatoes, mixing well. Transfer potato mixture to pastry bag.

3. Pipe potato mixture into mounds on prepared baking sheet. If desired, brush lightly with melted margarine.

4. Bake in preheated oven until potatoes are golden brown (the baking time will vary depending on the size and thickness of your mounds).

# Hasselback Potatoes

## with Homemade Sage Butter

This potato recipe has enjoyed great popularity in recent years. In my home, they've become a classic side dish for a holiday meal. They're easy to make and go beautifully with a little homemade vegan sage butter.

◆

## MAKES 8 SERVINGS

- Blender or immersion blender
- Small terrine or dish
- Baking dish

### Sage Butter

| | | |
|---|---|---|
| 3½ oz | soft silken tofu | 100 g |
| Pinch | salt (or to taste) | Pinch |
| Pinch | ground turmeric | Pinch |
| ⅓ cup | melted virgin coconut oil | 75 mL |
| 6 to 10 | fresh sage leaves, chopped | 6 to 10 |

### Potatoes

| | | |
|---|---|---|
| 8 | medium oblong potatoes | 8 |
| | Neutral vegetable oil or olive oil | |
| | Salt and freshly ground black pepper | |
| | Sage leaves, torn in half (optional) | |

1. *Sage Butter:* In blender (or using an immersion blender in a tall cup), combine tofu, salt, turmeric and oil; blend until smooth. Stir in sage.

2. Transfer sage butter to a small terrine and refrigerate for a few hours or until hardened. Serve cold on the side or use as a spread. (Do not cook.)

3. *Potatoes:* Preheat oven to 400°F (200°C).

4. Cut thin slices crosswise through potatoes, stopping about ¾ inch (2 cm) from the bottom. Place potatoes in baking dish, brush with oil and season with salt and pepper. If desired, tuck sage leaf halves between slices.

5. Bake in preheated oven for 30 minutes or until potatoes are golden brown. Serve each potato with 1 or 2 dabs of sage butter.

# Herbed Potato Waffles

Crispy on the outside, tender on the inside, these delectable potato waffles are a gourmet alternative to traditional potato sides! They're rather on the rich side, but after all, it's a holiday!

◆

## MAKES 12 WAFFLES

- Preheat waffle iron

| | | |
|---|---|---|
| 2 lbs | potatoes, peeled | 1 kg |
| ½ cup | neutral vegetable oil | 125 mL |
| 2 tbsp | chopped fresh parsley | 8 g |
| 2 tbsp | chopped fresh cilantro | 6 g |
| 2 tsp | salt | 12 g |
| | Freshly ground black pepper | |
| ⅔ cup | soy cream | 150 mL |
| ½ cup | plain almond milk | 125 mL |
| 2 tbsp | cashew butter | 30 mL |
| 1½ cups | bread flour | 200 g |
| | Additional neutral vegetable oil | |

## TIPS

If your waffles do not detach cleanly, or if they come apart, they may be either overcooked or undercooked. Do not open the waffle iron all at once, but detach the waffles, using the spatula, while opening the iron little by little.

The waffles can be reheated in the oven for 1 to 2 minutes if needed.

1. Place potatoes in a pot of cold salted water and bring to a boil. Boil until fork-tender, then drain well. Transfer to a bowl.

2. Mash potatoes with a fork, then stir in oil. Whisk in parsley, cilantro, salt, pepper to taste, soy cream, almond milk and cashew butter until thoroughly combined. Incorporate flour, a little at a time, whisking vigorously to prevent lumps from forming.

3. Brush waffle iron plates with oil. Deposit a large spoonful of potato mixture on each plate. Close waffle iron and cook for about 5 minutes. Open waffle iron slowly, using a silicone spatula to gently detach the tops of the waffles. Once waffle iron is open, use spatula to detach bottoms of waffles. Waffles should be golden brown. Transfer waffles to a plate and keep warm. Repeat with the remaining potato mixture, brushing plates with oil between batches.

## VARIATION

Omit the flour and step 3, and you have an ultra-gourmet recipe for herbed potato purée.

# Potato Kohlrabi Pancakes

Potato pancakes are popular in many different countries' cuisines.
In this recipe, I strayed from tradition and slipped in some
kohlrabi for an original seasonal touch.

## MAKES 4 TO 6 SERVINGS

- Preheat oven to 325°F (160°C)
- 2½-inch (6 cm) metal pastry ring
- Baking sheet, lined with parchment paper

| | | |
|---|---|---|
| 1 cup + 2 tbsp | grated kohlrabi | 150 g |
| 2⅓ cups | lightly packed grated potatoes | 400 g |
| ⅓ cup | cornstarch | 43 g |
| 1 tsp | salt | 6 g |
| Pinch | ground nutmeg (or to taste) | Pinch |
| Pinch | freshly ground black pepper | Pinch |
| 3 tbsp | soy cream | 45 mL |
| | Neutral vegetable oil | |

1. Wrap kohlrabi and potatoes in a clean tea towel and squeeze out as much water as possible. In a bowl, combine grated vegetables with cornstarch, salt, nutmeg, pepper and soy cream.

2. Place pastry ring on prepared baking sheet. Spoon a little vegetable mixture into ring and press down firmly. Lift ring and form another pancake nearby. Repeat until all the vegetable mixture is used up, spacing the pancakes evenly. Brush pancakes lightly with oil.

3. Bake in preheated oven until pancakes are golden brown.

# A Feast of Sweets

Snow White Layer Cake
94

Orange Carrot Cake
97

Cardamom Almond Kringle
98

Marzipan Stollen
101

Mince Tarts
102

Pepparkakor
105

Shortbread Forest
106

Chestnut Crème Brûlée
109

Mont Blanc–Style Panna Cotta
110

Citrus Mini Pavlovas
113

Glazed Pear, Caramel and
Chocolate Pavlova
114

Vanilla Raspberry Vacherin
117

Frozen Tiramisu Log
118

Glazed Citrus Meringue Log
120

Almond Lemon Meringue Log
122

Mango Cocoa Domes
125

White Chocolate Medallions
126

Chocolate Duet
Pecan, Pumpkin Seed and
Cranberry Medallions
Coriander and Olive Oil Truffles
129

Coconut Truffles
130

Filled Chocolates
133

# Snow White Layer Cake

This cake, delicately flavored with almond, vanilla and coconut, is the perfect base to decorate with fruits, chocolate, caramel or your choice of coulis.

◆

## MAKES 10 TO 12 SERVINGS

- Preheat oven to 350°F (180°C)
- Kitchen scale
- Four 7-inch (18 cm) springform pans or round cake pans, greased or bottoms lined with parchment paper

### Cakes

| | | |
|---|---|---|
| 10 oz | plain soy yogurt | 300 g |
| ¾ cup + 5 tsp | neutral vegetable oil | 200 mL |
| 1 tsp | apple cider vinegar | 5 mL |
| 1 cup + 6 tbsp | raw cane sugar | 270 g |
| ¾ cup | ground almonds (almond flour) | 75 g |
| 1 tbsp | baking powder | 15 g |
| 1 tsp | vanilla powder | 2 g |
| | A few drops almond extract | |
| ½ cup | plain soy or other nondairy milk | 125 mL |
| 3⅓ cups | all-purpose flour | 450 g |

### Icing

| | | |
|---|---|---|
| 2 | cans (each 14 oz/400 mL) coconut milk, refrigerated overnight | 2 |
| Pinch | vanilla powder | Pinch |
| | Confectioners' (icing) sugar | |
| 2⅔ cups | shredded coconut | 250 g |

1. *Cakes:* In a large bowl, whisk yogurt, oil and vinegar. Whisk in sugar and ground almonds. Whisk in baking powder, vanilla powder and almond extract until well combined. Whisk in milk, then gradually stir in flour. Stir well until batter is smooth.

2. Using a kitchen scale, divide batter into 4 equal portions by weight. Spread one portion of batter in each prepared pan.

3. Bake in preheated oven for 20 minutes. Unmold and let cool completely on a rack.

4. *Icing:* Open cans of chilled coconut milk and spoon solidified cream on top into a bowl (reserve thin liquid for another use). Whisk coconut cream with vanilla powder and confectioners' sugar to taste.

5. If necessary, use a wire cake leveler or serrated knife to level tops of cakes so they are completely flat on top. Place one cake layer on a serving platter and spread a layer of icing on top. Repeat with the remaining layers. Spread icing over top and sides of cake and cover with shredded coconut. Refrigerate until ready to serve.

# Orange Carrot Cake

Here, classic carrot cake is treated to a finish of vegan "cream cheese" icing, for a recipe sure to turn the entire family into vegan-dessert fans! Decorate the top of the cake as desired with grated carrots, fresh fruits and spices.

---

## MAKES 12 SERVINGS

- Preheat oven to 350°F (180°C)
- Kitchen scale
- 8-inch (20 cm) springform pan, greased
- Immersion blender

### Cakes

| | | |
|---|---|---|
| 3⅓ cups | grated carrots | 500 g |
| 4½ cups | all-purpose flour | 600 g |
| ¾ cup | raw cane sugar | 150 g |
| 4 tsp | baking powder | 20 g |
| 1 tsp | salt | 6 g |
| 5 tsp | ground cinnamon | 14 g |
| 1 tsp | vanilla powder | 2 g |
| 1 tsp | ground cardamom | 2 g |
| 1 tsp | ground coriander | 2 g |
| 3 tbsp | grated orange zest | 45 g |
| 1 cup | neutral vegetable oil | 250 mL |
| 1¼ cups | freshly squeezed orange juice | 300 mL |

### Icing

| | | |
|---|---|---|
| 14 oz | soft silken tofu | 400 g |
| 3½ oz | plain soy yogurt | 100 g |
| 3 tbsp | soy cream | 45 mL |
| ½ cup | melted unflavored coconut oil | 125 mL |
| 3 tbsp + 1 tsp | freshly squeezed lemon juice | 50 mL |
| ½ tsp | vanilla powder | 1 g |
| ¾ cup | confectioners' (icing) sugar | 150 g |
| 2 | packets (each 0.35 oz/10 g) stabilizer for whipping cream, such as Dr. Oetker Whip It | 2 |

1. *Cakes:* In a very large bowl, combine carrots, flour, sugar, baking powder, salt, cinnamon, vanilla powder, cardamom, coriander and orange zest. Add vegetable oil and orange juice. Using a spatula, blend mixture into a smooth batter.

2. Using a kitchen scale, divide batter into 2 equal portions by weight. Pour one portion of batter into prepared springform pan. Set remaining portion aside.

3. Bake first cake in preheated oven for 40 minutes. Let stand for 10 minutes, then gently unmold cake onto rack. Clean and grease the pan and bake second cake the same way.

4. *Icing:* In a tall cup, using the immersion blender, blend tofu, yogurt and soy cream. Add coconut oil, lemon juice, vanilla and sugar; blend again. Pour mixture into a bowl and add stabilizer; using a whisk or electric mixer, beat for a few minutes. Refrigerate icing for 1 hour.

5. Once cakes have cooled, if necessary, use a wire cake leveler or serrated knife to level tops of cakes so they are completely flat on top. Place one cake layer on a serving platter and spread a layer of icing on top. Place the other layer on top. Cover top of cake with a layer of icing and refrigerate. Serve with remaining icing.

# Cardamom Almond Kringle

You'll find crown-shaped pastry in several countries at Christmastime —
for example, *kringle* in Denmark and *kringla* in Sweden. Estonian *kringel* has
enjoyed enormous popularity online thanks to the *Just Love Cookin'* blog.
Here is a vegan *kringle* recipe made with cardamom, but you can substitute
your own favorite flavoring if you wish.

◆

## MAKES 8 PORTIONS

• Baking sheet, lined with parchment paper

### Brioche

| | | |
|---|---|---|
| ⅔ cup + 2 tsp | warm unsweetened almond milk | 160 mL |
| 2 tsp | raw cane sugar | 8 g |
| 2¾ tsp | active dry yeast | 11 g |
| 2¾ cups | all-purpose flour (approx.) | 375 g |
| | Salt | |
| 2 tbsp + 1 tsp | neutral vegetable oil | 35 mL |

### Filling

| | | |
|---|---|---|
| 2 tbsp + 1 tsp | muscovado sugar | 30 g |
| ¼ cup + 2 tsp | sliced almonds | 25 g |
| 1½ tsp | ground cardamom | 3 g |
| 2 tbsp | neutral vegetable oil | 30 mL |
| | Confectioners' (icing) sugar | |

1. *Brioche:* In a glass, combine almond milk, sugar and yeast. Let stand for 10 minutes.

2. In a large bowl, combine 2½ cups (300 g) flour and a large pinch of salt. Add oil and mix with your fingertips for a few minutes. Add milk mixture and mix thoroughly to form a ball of dough, adding just enough flour to prevent dough from being too sticky.

3. On a floured surface, knead for at least 5 minutes. Dough should be supple and very elastic.

4. Transfer dough to a clean bowl, cover with a clean tea towel and let rise in a warm, draft-free place (for example, in an oven that has been slightly preheated then turned off) for 90 minutes.

5. Knead dough for 1 minute. Roll out into a large rectangle, about 18 by 10 inches (45 by 25 cm).

6. *Filling:* In a small bowl, combine sugar, almonds, cardamom and oil.

7. Brush filling over dough, then, starting at one long edge, roll up dough like a jelly roll. Cut dough in half lengthwise and twist pieces around each other, forming a crown. Place dough on prepared baking sheet and let rise in a warm, draft-free place for 30 minutes.

8. Meanwhile, preheat oven to 350°F (180°C).

9. Bake for 20 to 25 minutes. Sprinkle confectioners' sugar on top before serving.

# Marzipan Stollen

Stollen is a traditional German sweet bread packed with dried fruits
and filled with marzipan. It's Christmas, concentrated!

◆

## MAKES 8 SERVINGS

• Baking sheet, lined with parchment paper

### Filling

| | | |
|---|---|---|
| 5 tbsp | raisins | 50 g |
| 6 tbsp | finely chopped dried apricots | 50 g |
| 1 tbsp | chopped candied orange peel | 10 g |
| 6 tbsp | hot water | 90 mL |
| 2 tsp | dark rum | 10 mL |
| 5 oz | almond paste (marzipan) | 150 g |

### Dough

| | | |
|---|---|---|
| 2 cups | all-purpose flour | 280 g |
| 2 tbsp | raw cane sugar | 24 g |
| 1½ tsp | quick-rising (instant) yeast | 5 g |
| ½ tsp | salt | 3 g |
| 9 tbsp + 1 tsp | plain soy or other nondairy milk, warmed | 140 mL |
| 2 tbsp | neutral vegetable oil | 30 mL |
| | Confectioners' (icing) sugar | |

1. *Filling:* Soak raisins, apricots and orange peel in hot water and rum for 15 minutes. Strain fruit thoroughly.

2. *Dough:* In a bowl, combine flour, sugar, yeast and salt. Add warm milk and oil, then mix to form a dough. Knead dough for 10 minutes. Incorporate dried fruit and knead dough again for a few minutes. Form dough into a ball, cover with a clean tea towel and let rise in a warm, draft-free place (for example, in an oven that has been slightly preheated then turned off) for 1 hour.

3. Preheat oven to 340°F (170°C).

4. Shape dough into an oblong and place on prepared baking sheet. Shape almond paste into a small cylinder the length of the oblong and lay it on top of the dough. Fold dough over almond paste to seal it inside and arrange, sealed side down, on baking sheet. Your dough should be shaped like a loaf of country-style bread.

5. Bake for 30 minutes or until loaf is golden brown. Let cool on a rack, then sprinkle confectioners' sugar over loaf.

# Mince Tarts

A quintessentially English Christmas treat, mince tarts are filled with mincemeat: minced dried fruit, apple, sugar and spices. A pretty snack for teatime, they will perfume your home with the magical aromas of Christmas.

## MAKES 30 TARTS

- 2¾-inch (7 cm) round fluted cutter
- 12-cup muffin pan, 10 cups greased
- Small cookie cutter

### Mincemeat

| | | |
|---|---|---|
| 1 | large apple, peeled and finely diced | 1 |
| 1 cup | raisins | 175 g |
| 1 cup | dried cranberries | 175 g |
| 4½ tbsp | chopped candied orange peel | 50 g |
| 4½ tbsp | chopped candied lemon peel | 50 g |
| 3½ tbsp | almonds, chopped | 30 g |
| 4 tbsp | muscovado sugar | 50 g |
| 1 tsp | ground cinnamon | 3 g |
| ½ tsp | ground ginger | 1 g |
| ½ tsp | ground nutmeg | 1 g |
| 3½ tbsp | vegan margarine, diced | 50 g |
| 1 tbsp | Armagnac, cognac or brandy | 15 mL |
| | Juice of 1 lemon | |
| 3 | sheets pie dough | 3 |
| | Raw cane sugar | |
| | Confectioners' (icing) sugar | |

1. *Mincemeat:* In a saucepan, combine apple, raisins, cranberries, orange peel, lemon peel, almonds, sugar, cinnamon, ginger, nutmeg, margarine, Armagnac and lemon juice. Cook over low heat for 20 to 30 minutes or until mixture becomes a thick jam.

2. Preheat oven to 300°F (150°C).

3. Using the round fluted cutter, cut 10 tart bases out of pie dough and lay them in prepared muffin cups. Top each with 1 tbsp (15 mL) mincemeat. Using the cookie cutter, cut 10 small stars or other shapes out of pie dough and lay a shape on top of each tart. Sprinkle a pinch of cane sugar on top.

4. Bake for 15 minutes. Let cool, then sprinkle confectioners' sugar on top. Repeat with the remaining pastry and mincemeat, letting pan cool between batches.

## TIPS

You can keep mincemeat in a jar in the refrigerator for 1 or 2 weeks — or for up to 3 months if you sterilize your jars. Don't hesitate to prepare it in advance so you'll have more free time during the holidays!

You can also freeze the baked mince tarts. They will thaw easily at room temperature.

# Pepparkakor

In Sweden, it just isn't Christmas without pepparkakor, the famous thin and crispy cinnamon and spice cookies. This oh-so-simple recipe easily goes vegan. Just find some cute cookie cutters and have fun!

◆

## MAKES ABOUT 80 COOKIES

- Cookie cutters
- Baking sheets, lined with parchment paper

| | | |
|---|---|---|
| ½ cup | raw cane sugar | 100 g |
| ½ cup | muscovado sugar | 100 g |
| 7 tbsp | agave syrup | 100 g |
| ⅓ cup | water | 80 mL |
| ⅔ cup | vegan margarine, cut into pieces | 150 g |
| 1 tbsp | ground cinnamon | 8 g |
| 1 tsp | ground ginger | 2 g |
| 1 tsp | ground cloves | 2 g |
| 1 tsp | ground cardamom | 2 g |
| ½ tsp | baking soda | 2.5 g |
| 3½ cups | all-purpose flour | 475 g |

## TIP

You can keep the dough in the refrigerator for several days and even freeze it (thaw it in the refrigerator for 24 hours before using it). The cookies will keep for 1 week in a cookie tin.

1. In a saucepan, combine cane sugar, muscovado sugar, agave syrup and water. Place over medium heat, add margarine and let melt. Remove from heat and let cool.

2. Transfer sugar mixture to a large bowl. Add cinnamon, ginger, cloves, cardamom and baking soda. Stir in flour a little at a time. Stir until dough is an even consistency (it will be sticky). Form dough into a ball, wrap in plastic wrap or parchment paper and refrigerate overnight.

3. Preheat oven to 350°F (180°C).

4. Unwrap dough and lay on a work surface covered with parchment paper. Using a lightly floured rolling pin, roll dough out into a thin sheet. Using cookie cutters, cut out dough. Place cookies on prepared baking sheets, spacing them evenly.

5. Bake, one sheet at a time, for about 8 minutes or until cookies are just slightly golden. Let cool on a rack.

# Shortbread Forest

Instead of a gingerbread house, make an entire forest of shortbread cookies of different colors and flavors. They can also be tucked into little gift bags as gourmet presents.

## MAKES 20 SHORTBREAD COOKIES

- Christmas tree cookie cutter
- Baking sheets, lined with parchment paper

| | | |
|---|---|---|
| ¾ cup | bread flour | 175 g |
| ¼ cup | raw cane sugar | 50 g |
| Pinch | salt | Pinch |
| | Your choice of flavorings and nut butter (see variations) | |
| ¼ cup | neutral vegetable oil | 60 mL |
| ¼ cup | plain soy or other nondairy milk | 60 mL |

### Variation 1: Green

| | | |
|---|---|---|
| 2 tsp | matcha powder | 4 g |
| 1 tbsp | cashew butter | 15 mL |

### Variation 2: White

| | | |
|---|---|---|
| 2 tsp | grated lemon zest | 10 g |
| 2 | drops almond extract | 2 |
| Pinch | vanilla powder | Pinch |
| 1 tbsp | almond butter | 15 mL |

### Variation 3: Brown

| | | |
|---|---|---|
| ½ tsp | ground cinnamon | 1 g |
| 1 tbsp | hazelnut butter | 15 mL |

### Decoration

Confectioners' (icing) sugar
Melted chocolate

1. In a bowl, combine flour, sugar and salt. Stir in desired flavoring. Using your hands, mix in nut butter and oil. Add milk and stir until dough is an even consistency. Form dough into a ball, wrap in plastic wrap or parchment paper and refrigerate for 30 minutes.

2. Preheat oven to 350°F (180°C).

3. Roll out dough and cut out cookies. Place cookies on prepared baking sheets, spacing them evenly.

4. Bake, one sheet at a time, for a few minutes, until cookies are golden on the edges. Let cool on a rack. Decorate as desired.

## TIP

For even baking, bake cookies of the same size. If you are making shortbread cookies of different sizes, it is better to bake each size separately.

# Chestnut Crème Brûlée

Chestnut cream dresses up simple crème brûlée for a light,
refined dessert to follow a filling meal.

## MAKES 6 PORTIONS

- Immersion blender
- 6 shallow crème brûlée ramekins
- Kitchen torch

| | | |
|---|---|---|
| 14 oz | soft silken tofu | 400 g |
| 1¼ cups | soy cream | 300 mL |
| 1½ tbsp | cashew butter | 22 mL |
| ¾ cup | chestnut cream | 180 g |
| ¾ tsp | agar-agar powder | 2 g |
| 6 tbsp | raw cane sugar | 72 g |

## TIPS

Chestnut cream (sometimes called chestnut spread) is a smooth purée made from chestnuts, sugar and often vanilla, and can be found in jars or cans at specialty gourmet food shops, the imported section of well-stocked supermarkets and online.

For an ultra-gourmet version, add a few pieces of candied chestnut just after pouring the cream mixture into the ramekins.

1. In a tall cup, using the immersion blender, purée tofu, soy cream, cashew butter, chestnut cream and agar-agar.

2. Transfer tofu mixture to a heavy-bottomed saucepan and bring to a boil, stirring with a wooden spoon to prevent mixture from sticking to bottom. Boil, whisking constantly, for 2 minutes.

3. Pour mixture into ramekins and let cool, then refrigerate.

4. Just before serving, sprinkle each crème brûlée with 1 tbsp (12 g) sugar and use torch to caramelize top.

# Mont Blanc–Style Panna Cotta

Inspired by the signature dessert of the iconic Angelina pastry shop in Paris, this recipe takes a few liberties with the original, but you can make the meringues and domes ahead of time and decorate them just before serving. Who said beautiful pastry needs to be complicated?

## MAKES 6 SERVINGS

- Preheat oven to 195°F (90°C)
- Pastry bag fitted with a medium round piping tip
- Baking sheet, lined with parchment paper
- Six 3-inch (8 cm) dome-shaped molds or bowls with rounded bottoms
- Pastry bag fitted with a small round piping tip

### Meringues

| | | |
|---|---|---|
| 6 tbsp + 2 tsp | aquafaba (see box, page 113) | 100 mL |
| 1²⁄₃ cups | confectioners' (icing) sugar | 200 g |
| 1 tbsp | arrowroot starch | 8 g |
| | A few drops freshly squeezed lemon juice | |

### Panna Cotta

| | | |
|---|---|---|
| 1 | vanilla bean, split | 1 |
| ¹⁄₂ cup + 1 tsp | raw cane sugar | 100 g |
| ³⁄₄ tsp | agar-agar powder | 2 g |
| 1¹⁄₂ tsp | cornstarch | 4 g |
| 1¹⁄₂ cups | Homemade Vegan Crème Fraîche (page 27) or vegan sour cream | 350 g |
| 1 cup | plain rice milk | 250 mL |
| 1²⁄₃ cups | sweetened thick chestnut purée | 400 g |

1. *Meringues:* In a bowl, using an electric mixer, beat aquafaba into foamy peaks. Add sugar and arrowroot; beat for 2 minutes. Add lemon juice and beat for 10 minutes or until meringue is very thick and shiny. Transfer to the pastry bag with the medium tip.

2. Pipe 6 meringue spirals of about 3 inches (8 cm) in width on prepared baking sheet. With the remaining meringue, pipe small meringue circles or sticks.

3. Bake in preheated oven for 90 minutes. Turn off heat and leave meringues in oven for 1 hour, without opening oven door.

4. *Panna Cotta:* In a saucepan, whisk together vanilla bean, sugar, agar-agar, cornstarch, crème fraîche and rice milk; bring to a boil, whisking constantly so mixture does not stick to bottom of saucepan. Boil, whisking constantly, for 2 minutes.

5. Pour panna cotta mixture into molds and let cool, then refrigerate for at least 3 hours. Meanwhile, place chestnut purée in the pastry bag with the small tip.

6. Just before serving, place a meringue spiral on each plate, then place an unmolded panna cotta dome on top. Cover dome with piped threads of chestnut purée. Decorate with a little crumbled meringue and meringue circles or sticks.

## VARIATION

You can make frozen Mont Blancs using scoops of vegan vanilla ice cream instead of the panna cotta domes. See Glazed Pear, Caramel and Chocolate Pavlova (page 114) for a vanilla ice cream recipe.

# Citrus Mini Pavlovas

Mini pavlovas have become my favorite dessert to serve at holiday celebrations. They're easy to prepare and always impress my guests when they learn that these light and airy concoctions contain no animal products.

◆

## MAKES 6 SERVINGS

- Preheat oven to 195°F (90°C)
- Pastry bag
- Baking sheet, lined with parchment paper

| | | |
|---|---|---|
| 6 tbsp + 2 tsp | aquafaba (see box) | 100 mL |
| 1²⁄₃ cups | confectioners' (icing) sugar | 200 g |
| | A few drops freshly squeezed lemon juice | |
| Pinch | vanilla powder | Pinch |
| | Vegan whipped cream | |
| 2 | grapefruits, cut into segments | 2 |
| 3 | oranges, cut into segments | 3 |
| 2 | handfuls sliced almonds, toasted | 2 |
| | Grated zest of 1 lime or lemon | |

1. In a bowl, using an electric mixer, beat aquafaba, 2 tbsp (15 g) sugar and lemon juice to the consistency of whipped cream. Gradually beat in vanilla powder and the remaining sugar until a stiff meringue forms. Transfer meringue to pastry bag.

2. Pipe 6 meringue "nests" on prepared baking sheet.

3. Bake in preheated oven for 2 hours. Turn off heat and leave meringues in oven for 2 hours, without opening oven door.

4. When ready to serve, place a meringue nest on a dessert plate, top with whipped cream and citrus fruit, then sprinkle with almonds and lime zest.

---

## Aquafaba

In 2014, Joël Roessel published his experiments with "chickpea whites" on his blog *Révolution végétale* (*Vegan Revolution*). Quickly renamed "aquafaba" (in Latin, *aqua* = "water" and *faba* = "legume"), this liquid that can be whipped like egg whites transformed vegan cuisine and is being used by chefs around the world.

To make aquafaba, save the liquid from a can of chickpeas (or the water from chickpeas you have cooked) and reduce it a little until it is a viscous liquid.

# Glazed Pear, Caramel and Chocolate Pavlova

Here is a double-layered pavlova with thin circles of meringue and tiny balls of vanilla ice cream.

◆

## MAKES 8 SERVINGS

- Ice cream maker
- Baking sheet, lined with parchment paper
- Melon baller

### Ice Cream

| | | |
|---|---|---|
| 2 cups | soy cream | 500 mL |
| 6 tbsp + 2 tsp | soy yogurt | 100 g |
| 7 tbsp | raw cane sugar | 85 g |
| 1 | vanilla bean, split | 1 |

### Meringues

| | | |
|---|---|---|
| 2/3 cup | aquafaba (see box, page 113) | 150 mL |
| 3/4 cup + 2 tsp | raw cane sugar | 150 g |
| 1¼ cups | confectioners' (icing) sugar | 150 g |
| 2 tbsp | arrowroot starch | 16 g |
| ¼ tsp | freshly squeezed lemon juice | 1 mL |

### Filling/Topping

| | | |
|---|---|---|
| 1½ cups | drained canned pear slices in syrup | 300 g |
| ½ cup | sliced almonds, toasted | 45 g |
| 2 tbsp | chocolate chips | 20 g |
| | Caramel topping | |

1. *Ice Cream:* In a saucepan, whisk together soy cream, soy yogurt, sugar and vanilla bean; cook, stirring, over low heat until sugar is dissolved. Let cool, then chill in refrigerator.

2. Churn mixture in ice cream maker according to manufacturer's directions, then store in an airtight container in the freezer for at least 5 hours.

3. Preheat oven to 195°F (90°C).

4. *Meringues:* In a bowl, using an electric mixer, beat aquafaba and cane sugar to the consistency of whipped cream. Add confectioners' sugar and arrowroot; beat for 2 minutes. Add lemon juice and beat for 7 minutes or until a stiff meringue forms.

5. Use a spoon to form 2 circles of meringue, about 10 inches (25 cm) in diameter, on prepared baking sheet.

6. Bake for 2 hours. Turn off heat and let cool in oven, with door partially open, for at least 1 hour.

7. Place one meringue circle on a serving plate. Using the melon baller, scoop vanilla ice cream into small balls and arrange on top of meringue. Cover with some of the pear slices, toasted almonds and chocolate chips. Repeat with the other meringue circle and the remaining ingredients. Drizzle with caramel topping and serve immediately, using a large knife to cut pavlova into individual servings.

# Vanilla Raspberry Vacherin

Here's a frozen cake I never thought I'd see in a vegan cookbook.
Its presence here is thanks to the invention of aquafaba, which gives
us a vegan way to make meringue.

◆

## MAKES 6 TO 8 SERVINGS

- Preheat oven to 200°F (100°C)
- Pastry bag
- 2 baking sheets, lined with parchment paper
- Ice cream maker
- 8-inch (20 cm) springform pan, lined with parchment paper

### Meringues

| | | |
|---|---|---|
| ⅔ cup | aquafaba (see box, page 113) | 150 mL |
| 2½ cups | confectioners' (icing) sugar | 300 g |
| | A few drops freshly squeezed lemon juice | |

### Vanilla Ice Cream

| | | |
|---|---|---|
| 3 cups + 3 tbsp | soy cream | 800 mL |
| ¾ cup + 5 tsp | rice cream | 200 mL |
| ¾ cup | raw cane sugar | 140 g |
| | Seeds from 2 vanilla beans | |

### Raspberry Ice Cream

| | | |
|---|---|---|
| ⅔ cup | raspberry coulis | 150 mL |

### Decorations

| | |
|---|---|
| | Vegan whipped cream |
| | Berries |

1. *Meringue:* In a bowl, using an electric mixer, beat aquafaba, 2 tbsp (6 g) sugar and lemon juice to the consistency of whipped cream. Gradually beat in the remaining sugar until a stiff meringue forms. Transfer meringue to pastry bag.

2. Pipe 2 flat circles of meringue, about 7 inches (17 cm) in diameter, on one prepared baking sheet. On the other sheet, pipe 48 short sticks of meringue.

3. Bake on upper and lower racks of preheated oven for 1 hour. Turn off heat and leave meringues in oven for 1 hour, without opening oven door.

4. *Vanilla Ice Cream:* In a saucepan over medium heat, whisk soy cream, rice cream, sugar and vanilla seeds until sugar is dissolved. Let cool, then churn in ice cream maker according to manufacturer's directions.

5. Place one meringue circle in prepared springform pan. Add half the vanilla ice cream on top, then place pan in freezer.

6. *Raspberry Ice Cream:* Add raspberry coulis to the remaining vanilla ice cream in ice cream maker and churn for 5 minutes.

7. Place second meringue circle on top of vanilla ice cream in pan and gently cover with raspberry ice cream. Let set in freezer for at least 5 hours.

8. When ready to serve, remove vacherin from freezer and unmold. Using a little whipped cream, attach meringue sticks vertically all the way around the side of the vacherin. Decorate top with berries and whipped cream.

# Frozen Tiramisu Log

A totally frozen variation on tiramisu that's perfect with coffee!

## MAKES 8 SERVINGS

- Preheat oven to 350°F (180°C)
- Baking sheet, lined with parchment paper
- Immersion blender
- Log cake mold
- Ice cream maker

### Cake

| | | |
|---|---|---|
| ⅔ cup | soy cream | 150 mL |
| 1 tsp | apple cider vinegar | 5 mL |
| 2 tsp | baking powder | 10 g |
| 6 tbsp + 1 tsp | raw cane sugar | 75 g |
| Pinch | vanilla powder | Pinch |
| ⅓ cup | neutral vegetable oil | 75 mL |
| Pinch | salt | Pinch |
| 1½ cups + 4 tsp | Khorasan wheat flour (Kamut) | 190 g |
| 1 cup | strong brewed coffee, cooled | 250 mL |

### Ice Cream

| | | |
|---|---|---|
| 3 cups + 3 tbsp | soy cream | 800 mL |
| ¾ cup + 5 tsp | rice cream | 200 mL |
| ¾ cup + 2 tsp | raw cane sugar | 150 g |
| | Seeds from 1 vanilla bean | |
| 3 tbsp + 1 tsp | neutral vegetable oil | 50 mL |

### Decoration

| | |
|---|---|
| | Unsweetened cocoa powder |
| | Grated chocolate |

1. *Cake:* In a bowl, whisk soy cream, vinegar and baking powder. Add sugar, vanilla powder and oil, whisking well. Add salt and flour; stir into a smooth batter.

2. Spread batter on prepared baking sheet in a rectangle slightly larger than the dimensions of the base of your log mold.

3. Bake in preheated oven for 15 to 20 minutes or until golden brown. Let cool, then cut cake into 4 to 6 long strips. Brush strips with coffee.

4. *Ice Cream:* In a saucepan over medium heat, whisk soy cream, rice cream, sugar and vanilla seeds until sugar is dissolved. Remove from heat and, using the immersion blender in the pan, blend in oil until emulsified. Let cool, then churn in ice cream maker according to manufacturer's directions.

5. Spoon ice cream into log mold, filling halfway full. Lay 2 or 3 cake strips over ice cream and press down. Cover with ice cream, then another layer of cake strips. Cover with ice cream and smooth the top. Freeze for at least 4 hours.

6. Unmold log and sprinkle entire surface with cocoa powder. Sprinkle a little grated chocolate on top.

## TIP

For an even more elegant touch, serve this tiramisu with a chocolate sauce.

# Glazed Citrus Meringue Log

This light and lemony version of the traditional ice cream log is made with yogurt and almond milk and decorated with mini meringues. It's divine without being decadent.

◆

## MAKES 6 TO 8 SERVINGS

- Ice cream maker
- Log cake mold, lined with parchment paper
- Pastry bag fitted with a small round piping tip
- 2 rimmed baking sheets, lined with parchment paper

### Lemon Ice Cream

| | | |
|---|---|---|
| 7 tbsp | raw cane sugar | 85 g |
| 1¾ cups | plain soy yogurt | 400 g |
| 2 tbsp | finely chopped lemon zest | 30 g |
| 6 tbsp + 2 tsp | freshly squeezed lemon juice | 100 mL |
| 6 tbsp + 2 tsp | plain almond milk | 100 mL |

### Meringues

| | | |
|---|---|---|
| 3 tbsp + 1 tsp | aquafaba (see box, page 113) | 50 mL |
| ¾ cup + 4 tsp | confectioners' (icing) sugar | 100 g |
| | A few drops freshly squeezed lemon juice | |

### Orange Cake

| | | |
|---|---|---|
| 6 tbsp + 1 tsp | raw cane sugar | 75 g |
| ⅓ cup | neutral vegetable oil | 75 mL |
| 1 tsp | baking powder | 5 g |
| 6 tbsp + 2 tsp | plain almond milk | 100 mL |
| 1 cup | all-purpose flour | 130 g |
| ¼ cup | candied orange peel | 42 g |
| 2 | oranges | 2 |
| | Additional plain almond milk | |
| | Citrus slices or segments | |

1. *Ice Cream:* In a bowl, whisk together sugar, yogurt, lemon zest, lemon juice and almond milk; let set in refrigerator for 10 minutes. Whisk again, ensuring that sugar is completely dissolved. Churn mixture in ice cream maker according to manufacturer's directions.

2. Transfer ice cream mixture to log mold, leaving at least ¾ inch (2 cm) of space at top of mold. Let set in freezer for 2 hours.

3. Meanwhile, preheat oven to 200°F (100°C).

4. *Meringues:* In a bowl, using an electric mixer, beat aquafaba into foamy peaks. Add sugar and beat for 2 minutes. Add lemon juice and beat for 8 minutes or until meringue is shiny and sticky. Transfer meringue to pastry bag.

5. Pipe small circles of meringue, about ½ inch (1 cm) in diameter or less, on one prepared baking sheet. Bake for 1 hour. Turn off heat and leave meringues in oven for 1 hour, without opening oven door. Remove meringues from oven and increase oven temperature to 325°F (160°C).

6. *Cake:* In a bowl, whisk together sugar and oil. Whisk in baking powder and almond milk. Add flour a little at a time, whisking until blended. Stir in candied orange peel.

7. On the other prepared baking sheet, spread batter in a rectangle slightly larger than the dimensions of the base of your log mold. Bake for about 15 minutes or until cake is light golden. Let cool, then trim cake to fit the base of your mold.

8. Peel oranges and cut into ½-inch (1 cm) thick slices, then cut slices in half.

9. Remove log from freezer. Ice cream should still be slightly soft. Cover ice cream with orange slices, laid close together. Place cake on top and press down lightly over entire surface. A little ice cream may rise up the sides. Check that surface of the cake is very flat, cover with plastic wrap and freeze until ready to serve.

10. Gently unmold log onto a serving dish. Brush milk onto flat side of meringues and glue them over surface of log. Garnish with citrus slices or segments.

# Almond Lemon Meringue Log

Inspired by the famous lemon meringue pie, this log is the perfect dessert for lemon lovers and guests who shy away from the traditional heavier log cake.

## MAKES 8 SERVINGS

- Preheat oven to 300°F (150°C)
- Baking sheet, lined with parchment paper
- Log cake mold
- Pastry bag fitted with a large fluted piping tip
- Kitchen torch

### Shortbread

| | | |
|---|---|---|
| 1 cup | bread flour | 140 g |
| ¼ cup | raw cane sugar | 50 g |
| 5 tbsp | ground almonds (almond flour) | 30 g |
| Pinch | salt | Pinch |
| 3 tbsp | neutral vegetable oil | 45 mL |
| 1 tbsp | almond butter | 15 mL |
| 5 | drops almond extract | 5 |
| 3 tbsp | water | 45 mL |

### Center Strip

| | | |
|---|---|---|
| 4½ tbsp | chopped candied lemon peel | 50 g |
| 3 tbsp | coconut cream (see tip) | 45 mL |

### Lemon Cream

| | | |
|---|---|---|
| 1½ cups + 1 tbsp | raw cane sugar | 300 g |
| 3 tbsp | cornstarch | 24 g |
| 2 tsp | agar-agar powder | 6 g |
| 1 cup + 6 tbsp | soy cream | 350 mL |
| 1 cup + 6 tbsp | freshly squeezed lemon juice | 350 mL |
| 6 tbsp + 2 tsp | neutral vegetable oil | 100 mL |

### Meringue

| | | |
|---|---|---|
| 2½ tbsp | aquafaba (see box, page 113) | 40 mL |
| ⅔ cup | confectioners' (icing) sugar | 80 g |
| | A few drops freshly squeezed lemon juice | |

### Decoration

Thin lemon slices

Toasted sliced almonds

1. *Shortbread:* In a bowl, combine flour, sugar, ground almonds and salt. Using your hands, mix in oil, almond butter and almond extract. Add water and continue to mix until dough is an even consistency. Form dough into a ball.

2. On prepared baking sheet, spread dough ¼ inch (0.5 cm) thick in a rectangle slightly larger than the dimensions of the base of your log mold.

3. Bake in preheated oven for 10 minutes. Let cool, then cut out a rectangle slightly smaller than the base of the log mold.

4. *Center Strip:* Crumble leftover shortbread, weigh out 2¾ oz (80 g) and mix with lemon peel and coconut cream into a thick paste. On a sheet of parchment paper, form paste into a cylinder the length of the log. Fold parchment paper over cylinder and use a rolling pin to flatten paste into a strip measuring about ¾ by ¼ inch (2 by 0.5 cm). Place in freezer to harden.

5. *Lemon Cream:* In a medium saucepan over medium heat, whisk together sugar, cornstarch, agar-agar, soy cream, lemon juice and oil. Increase heat to high and bring to a boil, whisking constantly. Continue whisking until a thick cream forms. Let cool.

6. Transfer two-thirds of lemon cream to log mold. Remove center strip from parchment paper and place in center of log mold. Add the remaining lemon cream. Lay shortbread on top and press down into lemon cream. Refrigerate for at least 8 hours.

7. *Meringue:* In a bowl, using an electric mixer, beat aquafaba, 2 tbsp (6 g) sugar and lemon juice to the consistency of whipped cream. Gradually beat in the remaining sugar until a stiff meringue forms. Transfer meringue to pastry bag.

8. When ready to serve, unmold log on a serving platter, decorate with meringue on top and use torch to brown meringue.

Decorate sides of log with lemon slices. Sprinkle almonds around the platter.

## TIP

For coconut cream, open a can of chilled coconut milk and spoon out 3 tbsp (45 mL) of the solidified cream on top. Reserve the remaining coconut cream and the thin liquid for another use.

# Mango Cocoa Domes

If you don't have a knack for pastry and none of your desserts turn out right, here is an impressive recipe that is foolproof and requires no baking — perfect if you need to come up with a dessert at the last minute.

◆

## MAKES 6 SERVINGS

- Food processor
- 2¾- to 3¼-inch (7 to 8 cm) metal pastry ring or cookie cutter
- 2 baking sheets, lined with parchment paper
- Plastic squeeze bottle or pastry syringe
- Six 2¾- to 3¼-inch (7 to 8 cm) dome-shaped molds or bowls with rounded bottoms
- Melon baller

| | | |
|---|---|---|
| 7 oz | speculaas cookies, broken into chunks | 200 g |
| 3 tbsp | melted coconut oil (unflavored or flavored) | 45 mL |
| 2 | cans (each 14 oz/400 mL) coconut milk, refrigerated overnight | 2 |
| 4½ tbsp | unsweetened cocoa powder | 25 g |
| 2 tbsp | confectioners' (icing) sugar | 18 g |
| 3½ oz | dark baking chocolate or dark chocolate couverture | 100 g |
| 4 cups | mango sorbet | 1 L |

1. In food processor, process cookies and coconut oil to fine crumbs.

2. Place pastry ring on one prepared baking sheet and fill with one-sixth of the cookie mixture. Carefully remove ring and repeat to form 6 cookie bases. Let set in refrigerator for 1 hour.

3. Open cans of chilled coconut milk and spoon solidified cream on top into a measuring cup to make ⅔ cup (150 mL), then pour into a bowl (reserve thin liquid and any extra coconut cream for another use). Whisk in cocoa powder and sugar. Set aside.

4. In a bowl set over a saucepan of simmering water, melt chocolate. Transfer chocolate to squeeze bottle.

5. On the other prepared baking sheet, draw fine designs in chocolate to decorate the domes. Refrigerate chocolate decorations to harden them.

6. Fill molds with mango sorbet and smooth tops. Using the melon baller, scoop out a hollow in the center of each mold, leaving about ½ inch (1 cm) border around the edges. Fill hollows with cocoa mixture. Smooth surface of molds and freeze for 45 to 60 minutes or until set.

7. Place a cookie base on each serving plate, cover with a sorbet dome and add a chocolate decoration on top.

# White Chocolate Medallions

I always make chocolate medallions for the holiday season. They're so easy to prepare and so delicious, it would be a shame to do without them. Here is a pretty white chocolate version topped with cranberries, caramelized almonds and coconut.

## MAKES 20 MEDALLIONS

- 2 baking sheets, lined with parchment paper

| | | |
|---|---|---|
| 40 | almonds | 40 |
| 1 tbsp | raw cane sugar | 12 g |
| 8 oz | vegan white chocolate, chopped | 250 g |
| 3 tbsp | dried cranberries, chopped | 30 g |
| 5 tbsp | shredded coconut | 30 g |

1. In a small skillet, combine almonds and sugar. Place over high heat and cook, stirring, to caramelize. Continue stirring until all almonds are coated in caramel.

2. Spread almonds on one prepared baking sheet and let cool. Chop almonds and transfer to a bowl.

3. In a bowl set over a saucepan of simmering water, melt white chocolate.

4. On prepared baking sheets, using a tablespoon, form chocolate circles about $1\frac{1}{2}$ to 2 inches (4 to 5 cm) in diameter. (Pour a little melted chocolate from spoon and use base of spoon to spread chocolate in a circle.) Place almond and cranberry pieces on top. Sprinkle with shredded coconut. Refrigerate until set.

5. Carefully remove medallions from baking sheets and transfer to an airtight container. If you have several layers, use parchment paper to separate medallions. Refrigerate until ready to serve.

# Chocolate Duet

◆

## Pecan, Pumpkin Seed and Cranberry Medallions

### MAKES 20 MEDALLIONS

- 2 baking sheets, lined with parchment paper

| | | |
|---|---|---|
| ¼ cup | pecans, finely chopped | 30 g |
| 2 tbsp | green pumpkin seeds, finely chopped | 20 g |
| 1 tbsp | raw cane sugar | 12 g |
| 7 oz | vegan dark chocolate (70% cacao), chopped | 200 g |
| 2 tbsp | dried cranberries, chopped | 20 g |

1. In a small skillet, combine pecans, pumpkin seeds and sugar. Place over high heat and cook, stirring, to caramelize. Transfer to a plate lined with parchment paper, separating pieces as much as possible. Let cool.

2. In a bowl set over a saucepan of simmering water, melt chocolate.

3. On prepared baking sheets, using a tablespoon, form chocolate circles about 1½ to 2 inches (4 to 5 cm) in diameter. (Pour a little melted chocolate from spoon and use base of spoon to spread chocolate in a circle.) Place pecan, pumpkin seed and cranberry pieces on top. Refrigerate until set.

4. Carefully remove medallions from baking sheets and transfer to an airtight container. If you have several layers, use parchment paper to separate medallions. Refrigerate until ready to serve.

## Coriander and Olive Oil Truffles

### MAKES ABOUT 20 TRUFFLES

| | | |
|---|---|---|
| 7 oz | vegan dark chocolate, chopped | 200 g |
| 3 tbsp | olive oil | 45 mL |
| 3 tbsp | hot soy cream | 45 mL |
| 2 tsp | ground coriander | 5 g |
| 2 tsp | confectioners' (icing) sugar | 6 g |
| 2 tbsp | unsweetened cocoa powder | 12 g |
| 2 tsp | coriander seeds, crushed | 4 g |

1. In a bowl set over a saucepan of simmering water, melt chocolate. Using a heatproof spatula, stir in oil. Stir in soy cream, coriander and sugar. Let cool, then refrigerate until set.

2. Form ganache into balls, roll in cocoa powder, then shape into cubes. Stick a few crushed coriander seeds on each truffle.

3. Place truffles in an airtight container. If you have several layers, use parchment paper to separate truffles. Refrigerate until ready to serve.

# Coconut Truffles

These little snowballs are dangerously delicious. The mixture of coconut, praline and white chocolate makes them utterly irresistible.

◆

## MAKES 15 TRUFFLES

| | | |
|---|---|---|
| 7 oz | vegan white chocolate, chopped | 200 g |
| 3 tbsp | soy cream, warmed | 45 mL |
| 1 tbsp | agave syrup | 15 mL |
| 1¾ cups + 1 tbsp | shredded coconut | 170 g |
| 1½ tbsp | praline paste | 30 g |
| 15 | shelled hazelnuts | 15 |
| | Additional shredded coconut | |

1. In a bowl set over a saucepan of simmering water, melt white chocolate. Whisk in soy cream to make a ganache. Remove from heat and stir in agave syrup. Let cool, then stir in coconut and praline paste. Refrigerate until texture is thick enough to be molded.

2. Form ganache into small balls, inserting a hazelnut in the center. Roll balls in coconut.

3. Place truffles in an airtight container. If you have several layers, use parchment paper to separate truffles. Refrigerate until ready to serve.

# Filled Chocolates

It's not always easy to find vegan filled chocolates. Here are two versions that are easy to make if you'd like to try your hand at homemade confectionary.

◆

## MAKES 10 TO 15 CHOCOLATES

- Small chocolate molds

| | | |
|---|---|---|
| 7 oz | vegan chocolate couverture or baking chocolate, chopped | 200 g |

### Speculaas Cream Filling

| | | |
|---|---|---|
| 3½ oz | speculaas cookies, coarsely crushed | 100 g |
| 3 tbsp | melted unflavored coconut oil | 45 mL |
| 3 tbsp | soy cream | 45 mL |

### Quick Praline Filling

| | | |
|---|---|---|
| ¼ cup | hazelnut butter | 60 g |
| ¼ cup | raw cane sugar | 48 g |

1. Temper chocolate or melt it in a bowl set over a saucepan of simmering water. Spread a layer of chocolate over chocolate molds. Remove excess chocolate. Let harden in refrigerator. Make a second layer of chocolate and let harden.

2. *Speculaas Cream Filling:* In a bowl, combine cookies, coconut oil and soy cream.

3. *Quick Praline Filling:* In a bowl, combine hazelnut butter and sugar.

4. Fill chocolates with speculaas cream or praline filling. Cover with a layer of chocolate to seal. Using a spatula, smooth surface and remove excess chocolate from mold. Let chocolate harden in refrigerator, then remove from mold.

5. Place chocolates in an airtight container or a recycled small chocolate box. Refrigerate until ready to serve.

# Festive Cocktails and Gourmet Gifts

### Festive Cocktails

Ginger Hibiscus Cocktail

Orange Cranberry Cocktail

**136**

### Gourmet Gifts

Dill, Black Pepper and Lemon Butter

Sun-Dried Tomato, Rosemary and Smoked Paprika Butter

Garlic and Herb Salt

Lemon and Spice Salt

Cinnamon and Vanilla Sugar

**139**

# Festive Cocktails

These colorful, sophisticated cocktails are not too sweet and have just a hint of bitterness. A little vodka or gin can be added for an alcohol-based aperitif.

◆

## Ginger Hibiscus Cocktail

### MAKES 6 COCKTAILS

| | | |
|---|---|---|
| 1 cup + 6 tbsp | chopped peeled gingerroot | 115 g |
| ⅓ oz | dried hibiscus flowers | 10 g |
| | Juice of 2 lemons | |
| 4 cups | sparkling water | 1 L |
| 3 tbsp | agave syrup | 45 mL |
| 1 | lemon, cut into thin slices | 1 |
| | Ice cubes | |

1. In a jug or large container, combine ginger, hibiscus flowers and lemon juice. Add sparkling water and agave syrup. Refrigerate for 1 to 2 hours to chill.
2. Strain into glasses. Serve with lemon slices and ice cubes.

## Orange Cranberry Cocktail

### MAKES 6 COCKTAILS

| | | |
|---|---|---|
| ¾ cup + 5 tsp | cranberry juice | 200 mL |
| ¾ cup + 5 tsp | freshly squeezed orange juice, strained | 200 mL |
| 2 tsp | freshly squeezed lime juice | 10 mL |
| 4 cups | sparkling water | 1 L |
| 3 tbsp | agave syrup | 45 mL |
| | Zest of 1 lemon, cut into thin strips | |
| 1 | orange, cut into thin wedges | 1 |
| | Ice cubes | |

1. In a jug or large container, combine cranberry juice, orange juice and lime juice. Add sparkling water, agave syrup and lemon zest. Serve with orange wedges and ice cubes.

# Gourmet Gifts

◆

## Dill, Black Pepper and Lemon Butter

| | | |
|---|---|---|
| ½ cup | vegan margarine, softened | 125 g |
| 1 tbsp | chopped fresh dill | 3 g |
| ¼ tsp | crushed black peppercorns | 0.5 g |
| | Grated zest of 1 lemon | |

1. In a bowl, using a small rubber spatula, break margarine into pieces and mash with aromatics. Transfer mixture to 1 or 2 sheets of parchment paper. Roll paper into a cylinder, then fold paper at both ends. Refrigerate butter to harden and preserve it.

## Sun-Dried Tomato, Rosemary and Smoked Paprika Butter

| | | |
|---|---|---|
| ½ cup | vegan margarine, softened | 125 g |
| 6 tbsp | finely chopped dry-packed sun-dried tomatoes | 20 g |
| 1½ tsp | dried rosemary | 1.5 g |
| Pinch | garlic powder | Pinch |
| | Sweet Spanish smoked paprika to taste | |

1. In a bowl, using a small rubber spatula, break margarine into pieces and mash with aromatics. Transfer mixture to 1 or 2 sheets of parchment paper. Roll paper into a cylinder, then fold paper at both ends. Refrigerate butter to harden and preserve it.

## Garlic and Herb Salt

| | | |
|---|---|---|
| 5 tbsp | sea salt | 75 g |
| 2 tsp | garlic powder | 6 g |
| 1½ tsp | dried sage | 1.5 g |
| 1 tbsp | dried thyme | 3 g |
| 1 tbsp | dried oregano | 3 g |

1. In a bowl, combine salt and aromatics. Transfer mixture to an airtight jar.

## Lemon and Spice Salt

| | | |
|---|---|---|
| 5 tbsp | sea salt | 75 g |
| 2 tsp | caraway seeds | 4 g |
| 1 tsp | ground cumin | 2 g |
| ½ tsp | smoked paprika or sweet Spanish smoked paprika | 1 g |

| | | |
|---|---|---|
| 1 tsp | dried lemon peel powder | 2.5 g |
| ½ tsp | crushed black peppercorns | 1 g |

1. In a bowl, combine salt and aromatics. Transfer mixture to an airtight jar.

## Cinnamon and Vanilla Sugar

| | | |
|---|---|---|
| 2 | cinnamon sticks | 2 |
| 1 | vanilla bean, split in half | 1 |
| 1½ cups + 1 tbsp | raw cane sugar | 300 g |

1. Place cinnamon sticks, vanilla bean and sugar in a jar. Seal jar, shake contents, then store in a dark area for 2 weeks.

# Index

**Library and Archives Canada Cataloguing in Publication**

Laforêt, Marie, 1983-, author
   The vegan holiday cookbook: from elegant appetizers to festive mains and delicious sweets /
Marie Laforêt.

Includes index.
Originally published under the titles *Noël Vegan* ©2015, Éditions la Plage (Paris)
and *Joyeux Noël Vegan* ©2016, Éditions la Plage (Paris).
ISBN 978-0-7788-0585-4 (softcover)

1. Vegan cooking.  2. Christmas cooking.  3. Cookbooks.
I. Title.  II. Laforêt, Marie, 1983- . Noël vegan. English.
III. . Laforêt, Marie, 1983- . Joyeux Noël vegan. English.

TX837.L37 2017          641.5'636          C2017-905237-3